DARE *TO* EXPLORE

12 Lessons On **Islam**
And How To Reach **Muslims**

Bible Study and Workbook

by **Samya Johnson**
with L. McAlister

Dare to Explore
© 2014 by Call of Love Ministries Publications

Graphic Design and Layout by:
S. Davis www.boomerangdesigngroup.com
S. Nelsen nelsengraphics@gmail.com

ISBN 978-0-578-07645-4

Versions of the Qur'an used are:
 • The Yusuf Ali text is based on *The Holy Qur-an, Text, Translation and Commentary.* Lahore, Cairo and Riyadh, 1934.
 • The Marmaduke Pickthall text based on The Meaning of the Glorious Quran. Hyderabad-Deccan: Government Central Press, 1938.
 • M. H. Shakir's translation of the Holy Qur'aan. Tahrike Tarsile Qur'aan, Inc., Elmhurst, 2001.

For more information, or to order copies for your church or group, contact:
Call of Love Ministries
Tel: 832-220-4040
Email: info@calloflove.org
Web: www.calloflove.org

P.O. Box 498698
Cincinnati, OH 45249 USA

Contents

Acknowledgments

We extend our gratitude to the brothers and sisters in Christ who volunteered their time and expertise to review and edit *Dare to Explore*.

C. Beckett (previous missionary)

M. Champagne (pastor)

B. Hyatt (scholar)

M.J. Johnson (ministry leader)

C. Michael (editor)

D. Palmer PhD (pastor)

G. Reed (editor)

May the Lord reward you abundantly.

Call of Love Ministries leadership team

About the writers

Samya Johnson was born into a Christian family in Beirut, Lebanon. At the age of six, in Sunday school, she experienced the new birth that Jesus gives. Samya spent her school and college years during the civil war in Lebanon. God saved her from actual death three times. Samya and her family suffered severe losses in that war; she witnessed friends who were killed, which left her embittered and terrorized. During her college years, God dealt with her brokenness and amazingly she was able to forgive and love the Muslims, who were considered intolerable enemies in her community. Healing took place when the Lord led her to work in a Christian radio ministry. Samya started corresponding with Muslim listeners, answering their questions about Christianity and getting to know them personally. She could see them, for the first time, as people needing Jesus, just like her. Through this ministry, Samya led many Muslims from all over the Arabic world to the Good News of the Gospel. She also helped them in their new journey as followers of Christ.

The last civil battle in Lebanon, which took place in 1989, destroyed the office and studios of the radio ministry, so Samya moved with her colleagues to a satellite office in Cyprus to continue the Lord's work. God expanded her ministry to include writing and presenting hundreds of Christian Arabic radio programs. Samya met her husband in Cyprus. They married in 1992 in Egypt where they lived and served together for seven years. In Egypt, Samya continued to write and present radio programs. She also translated into Arabic several English Christian books, which were published in Egypt.

The story that God has woven in the fabric of Samya Johnson's life is one of His glory shining through a broken believer who humbled herself before God to make His will her own. Samya and her family immigrated to the USA in 1999. Since then Samya has been heavily involved in training and educating the western church about Islam and how to reach Muslims. With the Lord's help and the use of television, radio, and publications, her ministry efforts include:

- **Dare to Ask** — Samya records daily one-minute radio spots aired on many Christian radio stations in America.
- **Dare to Love** — Samya is the host and executive producer of this 30 minute weekly TV program that presents truths about Islam and equips Christ followers with practical tools to reach their Muslim neighbors. There is no other television program like *Dare to Love* now airing worldwide.
- **The Simple Truth** — the Quran and the Bible Side-by-Side: Samya's most recent publication geared toward a younger generation was released August 2013.

L. McAlister grew up in the greater New York City area, in a Christian home, mentored by strong godly women in the church. She attended Grove City College in Grove City, Pennsylvania, and received a Master of Arts in Theological Studies from Gordon-Conwell Theological Seminary in 1992. Since then, L. McAlister has held a variety of jobs inside and outside of the Christian world, including work in a research library, international publishing, and with a data management company. Currently she works for Call of Love Ministries as a writer and researcher. While raising her three children she has been actively involved in children's and women's ministries wherever her husband's job takes them.

Introduction

Islam is the second fastest growing religion in the world. Almost one out of every four people worldwide is a Muslim. Most Muslims are victims of "Islam," the religion they are born into. Muslims desperately need to hear the Gospel message of our Lord Jesus Christ. Therefore, we have to reach them with the Good News of the Gospel. We also have an obligation to protect our children and grandchildren from the westernized version of Islam which tries deceptively to present a friendly and peaceful Islam. Muslims have a mission to Islamize the whole world because they believe that Islam is the only true religion. Knowledge about Islam and its true agenda sets us free from our fears and protects us from these false teachings. That is why *Dare to Explore* is an applicable study containing crucial material for every true follower of Christ.

Call of Love Ministries, with its founder and president M. Michael, who has been working among Muslims since 1988, present this first of its kind Bible study to the Christian church in North America. We pray that its effects will make a positive lasting change in the body of Christ and in the way we see Muslims and the religion of Islam.

Important Notes

Please read these notes before you start your first lesson

- For group leaders, additional information is found in the Leader's Guide Section.

- An accompanying video series for the twelve lessons to use with your group is available for purchase at calloflove.org.

- Each lesson should take between two to three hours of personal reading and study.

- Lessons eleven and twelve are different from the first ten lessons in their structure. This is intended to help you spend more time on the lesson itself.

- **Glossary:** The glossary at the end of your workbook explains Islamic and unfamiliar words used. These words are printed in *italics* in the lessons.

- **Books:** A complete list of the books suggested throughout the lessons can be found at the end of your workbook. We encourage you to order your books from www.calloflove.org to support our ministry.

- **Online Qur'an and Hadith resources:** Read three well-known English translations of the Qur'an and check Hadith references at quran.com and alim.org.

- **Free online resources:** Check the **Free Resources** page on www.calloflove. org, where you can download free e-books and articles about Islam. You will also find helpful material to give to your Muslim friend on the **For Our Muslim Visitor** page.

- **Questions:** Your group leader can email the writers of *Dare to Explore,* so please give your group leader your additional questions about the study in order to receive an answer with additional resources for further study.

- **Feedback:** We value your comments and feedback. Once you finish studying *Dare to Explore,* please go to calloflove.org and fill in the "*Dare to Explore* Evaluation Form" or fill the form we provided at the end of this book.

- **Additional readings for each lesson:** Download additional articles for your discussion group from our website.

And now, with open minds and receptive hearts, let us start our trip together.

Lesson 1

War

In the Bible and the Qur'an

Islam: The Beginning

Part I: The Arabian Peninsula before Islam

Jews, Christians, and pagans (those who practiced idol-worship) all occupied the nomadic lands of the Arabian Peninsula long before Islam appeared.

Since ancient times, idolatry had enjoyed a position of tremendous importance among the Arabs; each tribe worshipped its own specific idol. Generally, the idols themselves were statues made of metal or wood, or were simply shapeless masses of stone thought to be heavenly. Classical works on pre-Islamic idols do not mention any statues made from precious metals or gems, with the exception of Hubal, the idol of the *Quraysh* tribe into which Muhammad was born. Hubal's image was made out of solid gold and *carnelian* in the image of a man. He was the greatest member of the Arab *pantheon* and resided in Mecca inside the *Ka'bah*. Pilgrims came to his shrine from all corners of the Middle-East. Hubal, whose other name was Sin, and whose title was Al-llah (the god), was shortened to Allah before Islam.

Judaism

Over the centuries, many Jews had immigrated to the Arabian Peninsula due to persecution in their own lands. During the 6th century, several rich Jewish tribes, such as Khaibar, made the Peninsula their temporary home. However, in Mecca, the center of pilgrimage and economy of the Arabian Peninsula, Jews and Christians were only allowed to live in houses isolated at the desert's perimeter. This distance prevented the lords and nobles of Mecca from being exposed to either religion. Whatever they heard of Judaism or Christianity they obtained from monks or hermits who lived in the desert near caravan roads.

The Arabic translation of the Bible did not take place until AD 87.

Christianity

Christianity reached the Arab tribes from its base in Egypt, which was under Roman occupation. The colonial structure of the Roman Empire enabled Christianity to move from Syria and Palestine to the adjoining Arab tribe of Ghassan and the shores of the Euphrates. Unfortunately, the majority of the Arab tribes who converted to Christianity, such as Hirah, Banu Lakhm, and Banu Mundhir, also embraced additional religious cults, such as the *Ebonites*. Muhammad was exposed to these cults. This accounts for why there are misrepresentations of Christianity in the Qur'an such as a false trinity of "God, Mary, and Jesus," which no true Christian group believes.

The Arabs: Sons of the Desert

The sons of the desert who occupied the Arabian Peninsula were nomads who had no taste for settled life. They knew no kind of permanence other than their perpetual movement in search of pasture. The basic governing unit for their life was not the state but the tribe. Moreover, a tribe, which was always on the move, did not acknowledge any universal law, nor did it ever subject itself to any general political order. To the nomads, nothing was acceptable if it fell short of allowing total freedom for the individual, the family, and the tribe. The sons of the desert took the law into their own hands and conflicts were often ended by the use of swords.[1]

It was under these conditions that Muhammad was born and raised.

Part II: Muhammad

Muhammad: The Early Years

Muhammad's father, the husband of Amina, died before his son was born. Shortly before Muhammad turned six, his mother died and the young boy became the responsibility of his grandfather, Abd al Muttalib. Approximately two years later his grandfather also died, leaving Muhammad, now eight, under the care and protection of his uncle, Abu Talib. This uncle taught the young orphan how to tend flock for a living.

Muhammad: His First Marriage

Abu Talib, Muhammad's uncle, was poor and had many mouths to feed. It was necessary that he finds his nephew a job that would bring more money to the family. He learned that Khadijah, a widowed tradeswoman of great wealth, was hiring men of the Quraysh tribe to act as her agents. They would bid and compete in the market on her behalf and be rewarded with a share of the profits. Abu Talib asked her to hire Muhammad and to pay him with four camels and she agreed. That same year Khadijah, who was 40 years old, asked Muhammad, then 25, to marry her. He accepted and was faithful to her for over 20 years, until her death.

Muhammad: His Offspring

Muhammad and Khadijah had three sons and four daughters. The girls lived to become adults and took husbands. Fatima, the youngest, married Muhammad's nephew Ali. In bitter contrast, the sons all died young. It is not difficult to imagine the depth of Muhammad's anguish in an age and culture where daughters were sometimes buried alive whereas male descendants were cherished as the substance of life itself. Muhammad could not bear to be without a

---

Muhammad's "Birth Certificate"

Date of Birth: AD 570

Gender: Male

Place of Birth: Mecca

Tribe: Quraysh

Father: Abdullah, the son of Abd al Muttalib
(died before Muhammad's birth)

Mother: Amina, the daughter of Wahb from Zuhrah tribe

---

[1]Lewis, Bernard, *The Arabs in History*, Goodword Books, 2001.

male heir. When he saw a slave named Zayd Ibn Harithah offered for sale, he asked Khadijah to buy him and then immediately adopted him as a son. His name became Zayd Ibn Muhammad. Zayd lived under Muhammad's protection and became one of his most faithful followers and companions.

Muhammad: The Beginning of Revelation (AD 610)

Paganism in the Arabian Peninsula was slowly disintegrating. Conversely, Judaism and Christianity were flourishing, together with *Zoroastrianism* and certain *Gnostic* sects. Several preachers of monotheism had arisen and each had gained a following, but it was Muhammad who succeeded in *syncretizing* certain basic elements of Judeo-Christian faith and practices with native Arabian tribal beliefs.[2]

Muhammad would retreat into the cave of Hira for solitude. One day while asleep in the cave, a spirit (some claim it was the angel Gabriel) approached him and said, "Read," (sometimes explained as "recite"). Muhammad answered in surprise, "What shall I read?" This conversation recurred three times, with the angel alternately strangling and releasing Muhammad. The third time, the angel replied: *"Read in the name of your Lord, the Creator, Who created man of a clot of blood. Read! Your Lord is most gracious. It is He who taught man by the pen that which he does not know"* (Sura 96:1-5). Muhammad repeated the words after the spirit, who eventually withdrew after the verses became permanently engraved in Muhammad's memory. Terrified by this encounter, Muhammad believed that he had become possessed by Satan. On returning home he related the episode to his wife Khadijah, who reassured him that he was not possessed, saying, "Joy to my cousin![3] Be firm. By him who dominates Khadijah's soul I pray and hope that you will be the Prophet of this nation. By Allah, He will not let you down."[4] She was the first person to believe in Muhammad as a prophet and to encourage him to pursue his call.

Muhammad: The Meccan or First Period (AD 610 – AD 622)

Although his own tribe, Quraysh, did not accept him as a prophet, Muhammad gained some followers in Mecca as he called on the people to reject idol worship and surrender to the one god, Allah. During this period, the messages he was receiving from Allah in the cave were peaceful. Allah was instructing him to be patient with his opponents, to take the Jews and Christians as friends and to forgive his enemies (Sura 73:10, 2:129, 3:89). During this period, he tried very hard to make the Jews and the Christians believe in his legitimacy as a prophet.

[2]Arthur Jeffrey, *Islam: Muhammad and His Religion* (New York: The Liberal Arts Press, 1958), xi-xiv.
[3]Arab women called their husbands "cousins" because most marriages were between cousins. This is still true today in Muslim countries.
[4]R V. C. Bodley, *The Messenger, the Life of Mohammed*, Doubleday, 1946.

Muhammad prayed towards Jerusalem five times a day for many years after he received his "call," in order to be accepted by the Jews. But the Jews rejected him as a prophet and Muhammad was banned from visiting Jerusalem. Only then did Muhammad seek another place to direct his prayers. He set his eyes on Mecca, the idol-worshiping city of his people.[5]

For an in-depth look at the reason Muslims pray five times a day please go to our website and read "The Night Journey" article. www.calloflove.org

Muhammad: The Medinan or Second Period (AD 622 – AD 632)

In AD 622, after being persecuted by his own people, Muhammad escaped from Mecca to Medina. This event, called Hijrah (immigration), marked the beginning of the Muslim era, but it was not Muhammad who first commemorated that historical event. Instead it was Umar Ibn Al-khattab, the second *Khalif,* who in the year AD 639 introduced the *Hijrah* era (now distinguished by the initials AH, designating the Latin phrase *Anno Hegirae,* "in the year of the Hijrah"). That is when the Islamic count for the Hijrah calendar began (For example January 1, 2000 in the Hijrah calendar would be 25 Ramadan 1420 A.H.).

During this second period, while in Medina, Allah changed his mind and sent messages to Muhammad to fight and kill anyone who would not submit to Islam. Muhammad then began to teach his followers to oppress or kill non-Muslims. Generally, Jews and Christians were allowed to live freely, provided they paid a special tax. This tax was called *Jizya.* It sometimes reached an incredible ninety percent of the gross annual income of the family. Jews and Christians who refused to pay this extortionate tax would have to convert to Islam or be killed, as would non-Jews and non-Christians such as idolaters or pagans, who were not afforded even the option of paying the tax.

Oppression of Jews and Christians is taught throughout the Qur'an. One of the most commonly used and memorized verses among Muslims is the "Verse of the Sword," where Allah says:

> Fight those who do not believe in Allah, nor in the latter day, nor do they prohibit what Allah and His Apostle have prohibited, nor follow the religion of truth, [which is Islam that abolishes all other religions] of the people of the Book, [meaning the Jews and the Christians] until they pay the Jizya [the tax imposed upon them] with willing submission and feel themselves subdued. [with humiliation and submission to the government of Islam] (Sura 9:29).

---

[5]Norman Geisler, *Answering Islam: The Crescent in Light of the Cross,* (Baker, 2002), 77.

Muhammad waged over 25 battles during this second period. It is interesting to note that Allah ordered a portion of the war plunder, one fifth or 20 percent, to be allotted to Muhammad:

> *"and know that whatever ye take as spoils of war, lo! A fifth thereof is for Allah, and for the messenger [Muhammad] and for the kinsman (who hath need) and orphans and the needy and the wayfarer"* (Sura 8:41).

Muhammad: His Wives

After the death of Khadijah in AD 619, Muhammad had sixteen wives in addition to the slave girls who were captured in battles. However, even with all these wives, no sons lived to be his heirs or keep his name. (More will be discussed about Muhammad's wives in another lesson).

Muhammad's Death

"In AD 629, Muhammad led his army and attacked the men of the Jewish tribe of Khaibar while they were on their way to work on their date palms. Khaibar was a settlement defended by a number of forts spread apart from each other. One by one Muhammad's army took the forts. Finally, the last few surrendered to him. Muhammad had several of the leaders of the Jewish settlement beheaded. Many of the women and children were enslaved.

Some of Khaibar's residents made a deal with Muhammad. Instead of enslaving them, which would leave the rich orchards of Khaibar untended and unproductive, the Jews would give Muhammad half of all the harvest. Muhammad accepted the deal, with the stipulation that they could be expelled at his slightest whim. Years later, Umar expelled the last remaining Jews from Khaibar.

Immediately following the conquest of Khaibar a Jewish woman, Zaynab bint al-Harith, prepared a dinner for Muhammad and some of his men. Unknown to the Muslims she had put a poison into the lamb (some say goat) that was served at dinner. Muhammad ate some of the poisoned lamb. Several of Muhammad's men died after the meal. When asked why she did what she did, Zaynab told Muhammad: "How you have afflicted my people is not hidden from you. So I said, if he is a prophet, he will be informed; but if he is a king, I shall be rid of him." Muhammad ordered that she be killed right there and then. Muhammad died as a result of the poison three years later, in AD 632 at the age of 62."[6]

---

[6]Silas, *"The Death of Muhammad,"* Silas www.answering-islam.org/Silas/mo-death (accessed April 2014).

6

Answers from the Word of God

Side Trip: A True Prophet

What are the characteristics of a true prophet according to the Bible? Look up these passages and summarize what you have learned.

Bible Passage	My Summary
Deuteronomy 18:14-22	
Exodus 7:1	
Jeremiah 1:4–10	
Exodus 7:10–12	
1 Samuel 12:16–18	
John 1: 6–18	
Matthew 24:22–24	

Main Trip: War in the Bible[7]

Bible Study Passage
Read Joshua Chapter 6.

War is not absent in the Word of God, but at the same time it is not glorified as in the Qur'an. We read in the Old Testament that sometimes God used the Israelites to wage war against other peoples. These wars had specific purposes and geographic boundaries, but in the midst of these wars God provided a means of grace and mercy. In Ezekiel 18:21–23 God says "But if the wicked man turns from all his sins which he has committed and observes all My statutes and practices justice and righteousness, he shall surely live; he shall not die. All his transgressions which he has committed will not be remembered against him; because of his righteousness which he has practiced, he will live. 'Do I have any pleasure in the death of the wicked,' declares the Lord God, 'rather than that he should turn from his ways and live?'" He goes on in verse

---

[7]The writers chose this subject for the Main Trip of the first lesson because in defending the way Muhammad spread Islam — through war and submission by force — Muslims compare what he did with the stories of wars in the Old Testament. It is important for Christians to be ready to answer this question.

32 to say, "'For I have no pleasure in the death of anyone who dies,' declares the Lord God. 'Therefore, repent and live.'" **Repentance** and **life** are always part of God's plan. It is important to know that God did not allow His people to use these wars for personal gain or needless destruction. Let us consider these two examples.

1. Abraham

In Abram's day every man had to protect his own household and possessions. A prosperous man, Abram had 318 trained men, born in his household, to protect him and his family (Genesis 14:14). When two kings invaded the valley where Abram's nephew Lot lived, Abram used his own trained men to deliver Lot. On his way back from the battle Abram met the high priest Melchizedek, who said to him: "Blessed be God Most High, Who has delivered your enemies into your hand." (Genesis 14:20). Notice that Melchizedek did not rebuke Abram for what he had done, but rather attributed the victory to God. The Bible tells us in the same passage that Abram refused the spoils of war even though they were offered to him by his enemy. Abram did not go to war to become rich or to gain power, he went to redeem his family.

Later, Abraham (now with his new name) found himself on the brink of war with Abimelech. A conflict had arisen over the ownership of a well that rightfully belonged to Abraham, but Abraham wisely avoided bloodshed by negotiating with Abimelech (Genesis 21:22–34). Consequently he was rewarded by making a covenant with Abimelech which protected him and his descendents from future conflicts with Abimelech and his descendants. In this act, Abraham reflected God's character by being a man of peace. We learn from this father of faith that even in the Old Testament there was a place for war as well as for mercy.

2. Moses and the Israelites

In Exodus 23:22-30 God made a covenant with Moses explaining how He would fight for the Israelites: "I will drive them out before you little by little, until you become fruitful and take possession of the land." Notice that the Israelites had an active role to play in God's plan. God laid out the laws of war for His people, but He did not give them a free pass to wage war whenever they chose and against whomever they wanted (Deuteronomy chapter 20).

Why Did God Permit War in the Old Testament?

The story of the fall of Jericho in Joshua 6 is one example of why God permits war. From this story we can see two main reasons for God's decision to wipe out the people of Jericho:

> Read Joshua chapter 7 where Achan is stoned for keeping the spoils of war.

First, the severe judgment that was brought against Jericho and all of Canaan did not come because they were hindering God's people, it came because this was a people who were in total rebellion against God and in league with the occult. Artifacts from Jericho indicate rampant idol worship and the presence of Rahab the harlot in Joshua chapter 2 shows that prostitution was an acceptable practice. In addition, we read in Deuteronomy 12:29–31 that the people of Jericho were burning their own sons and daughters as sacrifices to their gods. This city's dwellers were far from blameless. The people of God were commanded not to be "ensnared to follow them" in worshipping other gods and Joshua commanded them to stay away from the accursed things. God used the Israelites to punish the people to whom He had given so many chances to repent, but He took no joy in the destruction of Jericho.

Second, God used the Israelites to reclaim the land that He had promised to Abraham. This land had been taken over by sinful tribes and nations while Israel was in captivity in Egypt, and afterwards, wandering in the wilderness. In Deuteronomy 30:5, God told His people, "The Lord your God will bring you into the land which your fathers possessed, and you shall possess it; and He will prosper you and multiply you more than your fathers." In Deuteronomy 31:3 He had promised them: "It is the Lord your God who will cross ahead of you; He will destroy these nations before you, and you shall dispossess them. Joshua is the one who will cross ahead of you, just as the Lord has spoken." It was God's plan that His people return to the land of their forefathers to worship Him in purity.

In spite of this, we should remember that although God allowed war in the Old Testament, He looked upon it as a grim and terrible necessity for the restraint and punishment of national sins. War was to be avoided if possible. It was never to be glorified or used for man's personal gain. What better example do we have than God not allowing David, "the man after His own heart," to build a house for the Lord because of all the blood David has spilled in battle?

> David said to Solomon, "My son, I had intended to build a house to the name of the Lord my God. But the word of the Lord came to me, saying, 'You have shed much blood and have waged great wars; you shall not build a house to My name, because you have shed so much blood on the earth before Me. Behold, a son will be born to you, who shall be a man of rest; and I will give him rest from all his enemies on every side; for his name shall be Solomon, and I will give peace and quiet to Israel in his days. He shall build a house for My name, and he shall be My son and I will be his father; and I will establish the throne of his kingdom over Israel forever." (1 Chronicles 22:7-10).

Christ's Teaching on Peace

Moving on to the New Testament, we see that Christ never commands His followers to spread the message of the Gospel by the sword. The gospel is spread through personal witnessing. Jesus specifically teaches His followers to love not only their neighbors but also their enemies: "But I say to you, love your enemies and pray for those who persecute you" (Matthew 5:44). This is obviously a call to love and forgive, not to fight and kill.

The Sermon on the Mount summarizes the heart of the Gospel of Jesus Christ and Matthew 5:9 is the core of that message: "Blessed are the peacemakers, for they will be called sons of God." The sons and daughters of God are peacemakers and they are blessed.

Does this mean that God's character changed in the New Testament? Certainly not, God is still just and holy, and He still punishes sin in the way He chooses. At the Day of the Lord, every people group, every country, and every person will give account for their sins. It is only because of His mercy and patience that sinners are still given a chance to repent.

"The Lord is gracious and merciful;
Slow to anger and great in lovingkindness"
(Psalm 145:8)

Probing Deeper

1. Try to list at least five words or phrases that mean "war" to you, and five that mean the word "peace." Be creative!

_____

_____

_____

_____

2. What is the difference between the first period and the second period of Muhammad's spread of Islam?

_____

_____

_____

_____

_____

3. War is used as a different tool in the Bible than it is in the Qur'an. Can you state at least two differences?

_____

_____

_____

_____

_____

4. How easy do you find it to love those who consider you an enemy—like the Muslims?

_____

_____

_____

_____

_____

5. Go back to Joshua 6 and read about the conquest of Jericho. Would you have trusted Joshua when he informed them of "the walk around the wall" plan? Does it seem logical? What crazy spiritual battle plan is the Lord calling you to carry out? How will you persevere in that?

_____

_____

_____

_____

_____

Rest on the Road

Use this space to talk to God. Express what you feel right now about Islam. Ask God to help you understand the Muslims more and more. Then, turn to your own spiritual battles and seek His power and wisdom.

_____

_____

_____

_____

_____

_____

_____

_____

_____

_____

DARE *TO* EXPLORE

Points of Interest

Bible Passages

- Deuteronomy 20
- Joshua 6
- Matthew 5

Books

- Mikhail, Labib. *Islam, Muhammad, & the Koran: A Documented Analysis.* Blessed Hope Ministries. (2000)

- Lloyd Jones, D. Martyn. *Studies in the Sermon on The Mount.* Wm. B. Eerdmans Publishing Company. (1989)

- Davis, Dale Ralph. *Joshua No Falling Words.* Christian Focus Publications. (2000)

Chapter Notes

"As far as it is known, there are no ancient non-Muslim sources on the life of Muhammad, Islam's prophet and founder. There are two main sources for a history of Muhammad's life, both of which are Islamic. While the Qur'an is not a biographical work, it does provide information into the life and mind of the founder of Islam. The two ancient biographies of Muhammad are *The Life History of Muhammad,* by Ibn-Ishaq (A.D. 768), edited by Ibn-Hisham (AD 833); and *The Expeditions of Muhammad,* by Al-Waqidi (AD 822). The evidences from these sources provide a picture of the life and history of Muhammad"[8].

8"Who was Muhammad? Founder of Islam and leader of Jihad," *Contender Ministries,* http://contenderministries.org/islam/muhammad.php (accessed April 2014).

Lesson 2

The Book

The Foundation of Our Faith

Foundations of Islam

Part I: The Two Esteemed Books of Islam

Muslims reject the Bible and embrace other books as the foundation of their beliefs. The Qur'an and the *Hadith* are the primary sources of their doctrines and theology.

1. The Qur'an

Who wrote the Qur'an? Is it the work of a singular person, or the compilation of several authors?

To answer these questions Muslims depend upon a secondary source, the Hadith, which was put together generations after Muhammad died. While the Qur'an does not explain its own origin, the official answers regarding its formation can be found in the Hadith. In this, Muslims utilize a form of circular reasoning: They prove the Qur'an by the Hadith and then prove the Hadith by the Qur'an!

From the Hadith: The Story of the Qur'an

From Hadith Al-Bukhari Vol. VI, No. 509 we learn the following things about the Qur'an:

1. Muhammad did not write the Qur'an, so there were no original manuscripts of what Allah revealed to him.
2. Some of the companions of Muhammad were killed in battle and whatever Suras (chapters) they had memorized died with them.
3. The first *Khalif* (successor to Muhammad), Abu Bakr, asked Zaid bin Thabit, one of Muhammad's personal scribes, to collect the thousands of fragments of the Qur'an (that had been written by Muhammad's followers from their memory) and arrange them into a manuscript.
4. Zaid hesitated because the task was harder than sifting through an entire mountain.

According to the Hadith, the task was difficult because:

- The texts were written on fragile materials, including palm leaves, stones, and bones.
- The texts depended on the faulty memories and sometimes false claims of men. (Hadith Volume VI, No. 523 and No. 527)
- There were conflicting versions of the Qur'an. (Hadith Vol. VI, Nos. 510, 514, 523)

For an excellent resource to compare different English translations of the Qur'an use **Quran.com**

- Allah caused verses to be abrogated or forgotten. (Hadith Vol. IV, Nos.57, 62, 69, and Vol. VI, Nos. 510, 511, 527, Qur'an Sura 2:106; 16:101)
- Muhammad himself forgot and missed various parts of the Qur'an when relating it to his followers. (Hadith Vol. VI, Nos. 558, 562)

Standardization of the Qur'an

In approximately AD 650, eighteen years after Muhammad's death, Islam had expanded beyond the Arabian Peninsula into Persia, the Mediterranean, and North Africa. By that time there were many different versions of the Qur'an spread all over the Muslim World. In order to preserve the sanctity of the text, the third Khalif, Uthman ibn Affan, ordered the preparation of a formally standardized version. This officially sanctioned project was based on the copy of the Qur'an kept by Hafsa bint Umar (one of Muhammad's wives). The unapproved copies used by Muslims in other areas were collected and sent to Medina, where, on orders of the Khalif, they were burned or boiled. The approved text continues to be the authoritative, universally accepted version of the Qur'an to this day. (Hadith VI, No. 510, Vol. I, No. 63; Vol. IV, No. 709; Vol. VI, Nos. 507, 510)

Attributes of the Qur'an

- It was revealed to Muhammad over twenty-three years, beginning in the month of *Ramadan* in AD 610.
- Muslims assert that it has miraculous poetic quality. Many modern readers of Arabic think it is poorly written.
- They believe the text is engraved from eternity on Allah's throne.
- It is written in ancient Arabic and Muslims believe that its meaning transcends translation. Versions of the Qur'an in other languages are called "The meaning of the Qur'an"; many verses are watered down and westernized so as not to offend the reader.
- The Qur'an mixes verses from the Meccan period (the first peaceful period of Muhammad's prophet-hood), and the Medinan period (the second period which was filled with jihad and fighting). This gives the text a contradictory nature.
- The Qur'an consists of 114 Suras, or chapters.
- The Suras are arranged by length, from longest to shortest, with no chronological or thematic order. Repetition is extensive.
- The Qur'an is slightly shorter than the New Testament.

> *Sura* literally means "picture," so each chapter is believed to be the image of what is inscribed on Allah's throne.

Factual Errors of the Qur'an

There are hundreds of mistakes in the Qur'an; these are just a few examples:

- **Theological Errors** — The Qur'an does not report correctly about what

Christians and Jews believe (Sura 5:73,75; 9:30).

- **Historic and Geographic Errors** — There are several errors concerning dates and locations. For example, the Samaritans were not at Mount Sinai with Moses (Sura 20:85-97).
- **Grammatical Errors** — Arabic scholars point out grammatical errors in Suras 2:177, 192; 3:59; 4:162; 5:69; 7:160; 13:28; 20:66; 63:10.
- **Scientific Errors** — The Qur'an asserts that the sun sets in a muddy pond (Sura 18:86) and that mountains never shake (Sura 16:15; 21:31; 31:10; 78:6, 7; 88:19).
- **Moral Errors** — Muhammad justifies marrying his daughter-in-law (Sura 33:36,38).
- **Mathematical Errors** — Differing reports as to whether creation took six days (Sura 7:51; 10:3) or eight days (Sura 41:9, 10, 12).
- **Chronological Errors** — The Qur'an puts contemporary Muslim vocabulary, which did not exist in Hebrew or in Arabic at the time, into the mouths of the prophets and patriarchs (Sura 2:140-142; 7:124,126).

2. The Hadith

Hadith means "narrative or report." It is the narration originating from the words and deeds of Muhammad, his wives, and his first followers. After the death of Muhammad, his followers started writing bits and pieces about what his life was like. Some were true while others were exaggerated tales. Hadith resources were evaluated and gathered into large collections mostly during the reign of Umar Bin Abdel Aziz during the 9th century.

The works of the Hadith are referred to in matters of Islamic Law and history to this day. Hadith narrations are categorized as *Sahih* (sound, authentic), *Da'if* (weak), or *Mawdu* (fabricated). Shi'ites and Sunnis have different sets of the Hadith. Today the Hadith is the second most esteemed book to the Muslims after the Qur'an.

Hadith

The most trusted collection of Hadith is *Sahih Al-Bukhari*. You can search the volumes of Hadith at www.alim.org.

Part II: Shari'a Law

Shari'a translated from the Arabic means "The Law of Allah." It is the religious code for living to Muslims. Shari'a refers to:

- The Islamic system of law; it dictates governments and courts.
- The totality of the Islamic way of life; it directs the social system.

Shari'a Law is derived from the Qur'an and the Hadith. Muhammad Ash-shafiee (AD 767–820), a Muslim jurist, laid down the basic principles of Islamic

law in his book *Al-Risala* (The Message).

Shari'a was adopted by the Ottoman Empire in the early 19th century, officially transferring the rule of law from the jurists to the governments.

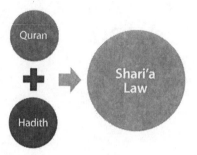

There are four main schools of Shari'a law: Hanbali, Hanifi, Maliki, and Shafi'i. Hanbali is the most conservative school of Shari'a. It is currently used in Saudi Arabia, Iran, Sudan, northern Nigeria, and among all Muslim extremists. All Muslim countries derive their law for secular courts from the Shari'a.

Examples of Severe Codes of Punishment for Lawbreakers Under Shari'a Law

- Stealing — Amputation of Hands (Qur'an Sura 5:33, 38).
- Drinking — Eighty Lashes (Hadith Al-Bukhari, Punishments, Nos. 6774-6775).
- Adultery — Stoning to death (Hadith Al-Bukhari, Punishments, Nos. 6831 and 6833).
- Abandoning Islam — Death (Hadith Al-Bukhari, Dealing With Apostates, No. 17).
- Life for a life, eye for an eye — Qur'an Sura 5:45 (Except in honor killing, or killing a non-Muslim).

In 2008, the United Kingdom formally recognized the first Shari'a arbitration tribunals. As of this writing in 2014 there are 85 officially recognized tribunals. These tribunals are given authority to govern marriage, divorce, business contracts, and inheritance issues to make legally binding decisions if both parties agree to have the matter resolved by the tribunal.

While this is the official stance in the UK, the reality sometimes proves to be much different. The number of unsanctioned Shari'a tribunals or courts is unknown, and the truly unknown factor in all of it is if both parties can ever really voluntarily agree to have their problem mediated by a Shari'a tribunal. In a religion that considers women half in standing to men, is her submission to the tribunal ever of her own free will?

In the US, as of 2014, the battle continues between Muslims and states to gain access to Shari'a law in the court system. However, Muslims do practice Shari'a law within the walls of the mosque.

Answers from the Word of God

Side Trip: God's Nature

What does each of these verses say about God's nature? Is it progressive? Does it change? Does it retain its fundamental principles, or does it contradict itself? Find out for yourself.

Bible Verse:	God's Nature Revealed:
Isaiah 40:28	
Psalm 102:25-28	
Malachi 3:6	
Hebrews 13:8	
James 1:17	

Main Trip: The Only Source of Truth

Bible Study Passage
II Timothy 3:16

> "All Scripture is inspired by God and profitable for teaching, for reproof, for correction, for training in righteousness."

This Amazing Book!
The Bible is composed of sixty-six books and was written by about forty different authors of various backgrounds and ethnicities. They lived within a period of about 1,600 years—yet they present one unified, continuous message. The Bible's writers came from many walks of life. They were kings, peasants, philosophers, fishermen, herdsmen, poets, statesmen, scholars, soldiers, priests, prophets, a tax collector, a tent-making rabbi, and a Gentile doctor. The Bible was written in three different languages (Hebrew, Aramaic, and Greek), in a variety of types of literature—history, law, poetry, parables, biography, letters, and prophecy. Together these sixty-six books contain the inspired story of God's work throughout history. It is amazing that God would use all of these

people, writing methods, and languages as tools to reveal one harmonious text that discloses His message of love and salvation to humanity.

But how can we be sure that the Bible is the one and only source to learn about God? Let's explore what facts are available to prove the Bible's authority and inspiration. First we will look directly to the Word of God to see how it can prove itself and then we will consult some outside resources. Let's get started.

1. The Word of God Proves Itself

The Word of God includes God's own words. Over 3,800 times the Bible expressly states that it is the Word of God. The first five books of the Bible, also called the Pentateuch, or the Five Scrolls, use the phrase "the Word of the Lord" over 420 times. In addition to this, God Himself speaks in the first person over and over again to prophets (Joel 1:1), priests (Luke 1:11–20), kings (Daniel 4:19–35), and even ordinary people (Judges 13:2–8).

God also addresses people groups and entire cities. "Comfort, comfort my people, says your God. Speak tenderly to Jerusalem, and cry to her that her warfare is ended, that her iniquity is pardoned that she has received from the Lord's hand double for all her sins" (Isaiah 40:1–3, NIV).

God speaks directly to us with His own words through the Scripture, as we read in II Peter 1:20-21: "Above all, you must understand that no prophecy of Scripture came about by the prophet's own interpretation of things. For prophecy never had its origin in the human will, but prophets, though human, spoke from God as they were carried along by the Holy Spirit" (NIV).

Jesus affirms the trustworthiness of the Old Testament throughout His ministry. Jesus' references to the Old Testament affirm that it is the inspired Word of God.

- Jesus continually cites Old Testament people and events. Examples: people — Abel (Matthew 23:35), Abraham (Matthew 8:11); events — The Flood (Matthew 24:37-39) Jonah (Matthew 12:40-41).
- Jesus affirms the ethical integrity of the Old Testament when He speaks of love (Matthew 22:37-40), marriage (Matthew 19:4-6), and many other subjects.
- Jesus affirms Old Testament truths such as resurrection and grace (Mark 12:26–27) and the end times (Matthew 24:15).
- Jesus frequently uses the Old Testament as a reference to refute the Pharisees (Mark 7:5–13, Luke 13:31–35). In fact, nearly one out of every ten verses in the New Testament is a quotation or clear allusion to the Old Testament.

Prophecies are fulfilled. The Old Testament books in the Bible (all of them written between 1450 BC and 430 BC) contain hundreds of prophecies about an "Anointed One" (Messiah in Hebrew) who would arrive in their future. All of these prophecies from the Old Testament have been fulfilled, except the ones that concern His second coming. The completion of these prophecies confirms the authenticity of the Bible.

Check some Old Testament prophecies that were fulfilled. You can find more on this website: http://www.clarifyingchristianity.com/m_prophecies.shtml

Theme	Old Testament Prophecy	New Testament Fulfillment
John the Baptist	Malachi 3:1	Matthew 11:10
The Virgin Birth of Jesus	Isaiah 7:14	Matthew 1:23
Bethlehem as the Birthplace	Micah 5:2	Matthew 2:6
Jesus' Death	Psalms 34:20, Exodus 12:46	John 19:36
Jesus' Resurrection	Isaiah 53:11-12	Mark 16:1-20

2. Outside Resources that Confirm the Bible's Authenticity

Authenticity of the Manuscripts. The New Testament is comparable to other texts from ancient times whose historicity is seldom called into question. Historian F. F. Bruce comments:

> "The evidence for our New Testament writings is ever so much greater than the evidence for many writings of classical authors, the authenticity of which no one dreams of questioning. And if the New Testament were a collection of secular writings, their authenticity would generally be regarded as beyond all doubt. There is evidence of 4000 Greek manuscripts of the New Testament from before 1200 AD and full manuscripts from as early as 350 A.D. There are fragments from much earlier than that. There is more documentation of a purely historical nature for the reliability of the Gospels than there is for Napoleon's battle at Waterloo, which no one has questioned."[1]

---

[1]F.F. Bruce, *The New Testament Documents: Are They Reliable?* (Grand Rapids: Wm. B. Eerdmans Publishing Company, 1998) 10.

First and Second Century Church Fathers. During the first and second centuries after Christ, Christian leaders, referred to as the Church Fathers, quoted the New Testament extensively in their personal writings. Examples:

- Clement of Alexandria, AD 150–AD 212, has 2,406 quotations from all but three books of the New Testament.
- Tertullian, AD 160–AD 220, who was an elder of the church in Carthage, quotes the New Testament 7,258 times.
- Others: Justin Martyr, 330 quotations; Irenaeus, 1,819 quotations; Origen, 17,922 quotations; Hippolytus, 1,378 quotations; and Eusebius, 5,176 quotations. All together, this adds up to a total of 36,289 quotations of the New Testament.

What is interesting and significant about these numerous quotations of the New Testament is that if all the manuscripts of the New Testament in existence were destroyed, you would be able to reproduce all but eleven verses of the New Testament from these quotations of the Church Fathers.

In addition to internal evidence recognition by the church fathers, evidence from different areas of sciences, such as geology, physics, archaeology, and biology, confirm the authenticity of the Bible. You can learn more about them in some of the resources we provide at the end of this lesson.

Because we have faith that the Bible is the inspired Word of God we can have confidence in the accuracy and consistency of the instruction we receive from it. The fact that we did not live when the revelations and teachings first came, should not leave us empty and questioning. We have a sure guide, a solid foundation, and this ought to motivate us to read, search, and study the Scriptures unceasingly. The Bible is the exclusive book that we can boldly call "The Word of God".

> "O how I love Your law!
> It is my meditation all the day"
> (Psalm 119:97)

Probing Deeper

1. List books, people, TV programs, movies or magazines that you really like
and have liked (including the ones from when you were a kid).

_____

_____

_____

_____

_____

2. What are the two main books of Islam? How do they differ?

_____

_____

_____

_____

_____

3. Can we compare Shari'a law in any way with what Jesus taught us?

_____

_____

_____

_____

_____

4. List some ways that the Bible proves itself as the Word of God.

_____

_____

_____

_____

_____

5. Where do you derive your ethics, moral standards, and spiritual truths from? Are they obtained from the list you wrote in question one or from the Word of God? Stop and think for a few minutes about this question and try to acknowledge the foundation of your beliefs.

_____

_____

_____

_____

_____

Rest on the Road

Do you love the Word of God? Do you yearn to read and study it every day? If not, ask God to put this desire in you. Seek to have a deeper knowledge of Him so you can live the life God has always intended for you.

_____

_____

_____

_____

_____

_____

_____

_____

_____

_____

Points of Interest

Bible Passages

- Isaiah 35
- Psalm 119

Books

- Bramsen, Paul D. *One God One Message.* Xulon. (2007)
- Strobel, Lee. *The Case for Christ.* Zondervan Publishing House. (1998)
- Bruce, F.F. *The New Testament Documents: Are They Reliable?* Wm. B. Eerdmans Publishing Company. (2003)

Web Sites

- Michael D. Marlowe. Bible Research: Internet Resources for Students of Scripture. http://www.bible-researcher.com (accessed April 2014)
- Answering Islam: A Christian-Muslim Dialog. Textual Variants of the Qur'an. http://www.answering-islam.org/Quran/Text/ (accessed April 2014)
- *Answering Islam: A Christian-Muslim Dialog.* Introduction to the Index of Hadith. http://www.answering-islam.org/Silas/indexintro.htm (accessed April 2014)
- Website to search and compare Hadith. http://www.alim.org/ (accessed June 2014)

Lesson 3

A Missionary Heart

*Mission of Islam,
Great Commission of Jesus*

Islam: Sects and Mission

Part I: Islam after Muhammad

History tells us that the twelve months following Muhammad's death were spent in bitter bloody battles to subdue the Arab tribes who had renounced their religious views. However, Islam continued to grow, led by the Khalifs (i.e., successors) elected by the closest followers of Muhammad. Muhammad's successors during that period (AD 632–AD 656) were Abu Bakr, Umar ibn al-Khattab, Uthman ibn Affan, and Ali ibn Abi Taleb. Under this new leadership jihad continued much the same as it had under Muhammad. In AD 634 the Islamic military force advanced into Palestine and Syria where they defeated the Byzantine armies at the Yarmouk River in AD 636. Following this event, Muslims marched to conquer North Africa as well as Jerusalem. After the assassinations of the first three Khalifs, only Ali was left as the last of the four rightly appointed Khalifs.

Muhammad's Successors *Khalifs*

FIRST KHALIF	SECOND KHALIF	THIRD KHALIF	SHIITE SECT ALI IBN ABI TALEB
ABU BAKR 632-634 AISHA'S FATHER	UMAR 634-644	UTHMAN 644-656	SUNNI SECT ABU BAKR AISHA'S FATHER

The Beginning of Sects
AD 656-661 — Ali & Aisha, The Battle of the Camel

Two well-known leaders, Talha ibn Ubaydillah and Al-Zubair Al-Zuhri, with the support of Aisha (Muhammad's youngest and most beloved wife), rebelled against Ali (Muhammad's nephew and the husband of Fatima, Muhammad's daughter). The resulting "Battle of the Camel," taking its name from the beast Aisha rode throughout the battle, saw 10,000 Muslims slaughtered. Ali and his troops won, but he was ultimately assassinated by one of his disillusioned followers.

After the death of Ali, his son al-Hassan surrendered his Khalifship to Mu'awiya, the ruler of Syria and Egypt. Al-Hussein, Ali's other son, together with most of his family, was slain under the reign of Mu'awayia's son at the battle of Kerbela, which is more aptly described as an assassination than a battle.

This event triggered a split in Islam. Those who sided with Ali and his sons declared that Ali and his family were the only true Khalifs because of their relationship to Muhammad. This group called themselves Shiites (meaning followers). Those who stood against the Shiites were the Sunnis (meaning people of the path). The Sunnis became the largest sect of Islam followed by the Shiites.

To this day the Shiites remember the loss of Hassan and Hussein in the city of Karbela on the day of Ashoura'a, an occasion they mark annually mourning the death of Ali's two sons. To commemorate the event they wound themselves, scream, reenact the battle, and dance to the cries of war and death. Karbela, now a modern city in Iraq, still welcomes hundreds of thousands of pilgrims attending this event every year during Ashoura'a.

Major Current Islamic Sects

According to tradition, Muhammad predicted that his followers would become divided into seventy three sects, every one of whom would go to hell, except one sect, the one who held the tenets that he and his companions professed (Hadith Mishkat I, pp. 169–170). However, the current number of Islamic sects is above 150, far exceeding Muhammad's prediction.[1]

The Two Main Sects of Islam

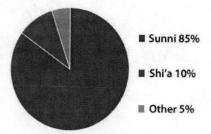

- **The Sunnis** — Meaning: "People of the Path." Over 85% of Muslims. These are Muslims who acknowledge the first four Khalifs to have been the rightful successors of Muhammad. The Sunnis are by far the largest group among the sects. Their spiritual centers are al-Azhar University in Cairo, Egypt, and the University of Medina, Saudi Arabia. Sunnis are spread all over the world and dominate most Islamic countries such as Egypt, Iraq, and Indonesia.

- **The Shi'a or Shiites** — Meaning: "Followers" (of Ali). Over 10% of Muslims. The *Shi'a* believe that Ali, the nephew and son-in-law of Muhammad, was the first rightful Khalif, and that his sons, Hassan and Hussein, should have succeeded him. Shiites have a saying, "Ali only". According to tradition, the twelfth in hereditary line of Ali, Imam-al-Mahdi (a kind of Messiah), is still alive and in hiding. He is expected to appear before the Day of Judgment. The center of Shi'a activity is in Iran, where the Ayatollah ("sign of Allah") Khomeini established the base for a Shiite Islamic missionary force. This fundamentalist movement is felt in almost every corner of the globe today. Shi'a Muslims are a majority in Iran, Lebanon, Pakistan, Syria, and in the U.S. Detroit.

The Wahhabis — Abd'ul Wahhabi, a diligent scholar of Islam in Mecca, Saudi Arabia, and Basra and Baghdad, Iraq, was born in AD 1691. His ultimate goal was the conversion of the whole world to Islam. The battle cry of the Wahhabi was "Kill and strangle all infidels, who give companions to Allah."[2] In the early 19th century a forceful reform took place in Mecca and the *Wahhabi*

[1]*Dictionary of Islam.* (Kazi Publications, 2007) 567–569.
[2]Contender Ministries, The Sects of Islam. http://contenderministries.org/islam/divisions.php (accessed April 2014).

school was revived. As part of this reform, all the people were driven with whips to attend the five daily prayers and women were forced to wear the full burqa in public. Today the Wahhabi influence is still a strong presence in Saudi Arabia and Northern India. Many influential Muslims, such as Osama Bin-laden are from this sect.

The Sufis — This sect is the mystical expression of Islam. It incorporates a distinct Hindu element in its teaching and practices. Most Muslims do not view *Sufis* as true Muslims. Sufis, being less orthodox, generally seem to be much more open to the Gospel than members of most other Muslim sects.

Folk Islam — This is the most popular form of religious adherence in Islam. It would be wrong to call this a sect, because it operates within Islam and is sanctioned by it. Folk Islam is a mixture of Islamic practices and occultism. Over 90% of Muslims practice it on some level.

Through Folk Islam, witchcraft, omens, sorcery, incantation, and other occult practices are widespread in all Muslims countries. Muslim Imams or Sheiks are usually the ones who imitate their prophet by practicing occultism. The Bible condemns such practices altogether: "There shall not be found among you anyone who… uses divination, one who practices witchcraft, or one who interprets omens, or a sorcerer, or one who casts a spell, or a medium, or a spiritist, or one who calls up the dead. For whoever does these things is detestable to the Lord" (Deuteronomy 18:10-12).

The Nation of Islam — The Nation of Islam is a sect of Islam centered in the United States. Its founder, Wallace D. Fard (c. 1877–1934), was a traveling salesman who gathered followers during the Depression among the poverty stricken African-Americans of Detroit, Michigan. Under Elijah Muhammad, Fard's successor, and later, under Malcolm X, the movement gained international prominence. The Nation of Islam's ultimate goal is the raising of the moral, social, and economic standing of non-whites, but in recent years the Nation of Islam has been working closely with Arab Muslims to spread Islam in America, especially in prisons. For further information on the Nation of Islam, go to http://www.beliefnet.com/Faiths/Nation-of-Islam/index.aspx

Other known sects: The Ahmadiyyas, the Mutazilites, the Baha'is, the Druz, the Black Muslims.

Part II: Islam's Mission in the West

Spread of Islam in America

The conquest of Islam is being felt today in European countries such as England, Holland, France, Sweden, and Germany, and in the past two decades Muslims have been focusing on North America. Islamic nations in the Middle East are spending a great deal of effort and money to Islamize the West.

The Muslim population in North America is 10-12 million. If the growth of Islam continues as it has in the past twenty years, by the year 2020 the number of Muslims in America will at least double.

Muslims in America are grouped as follows:

30% African-American

25% Arab origin

33% Asian (India, Pakistan)

3% African

2% European

1% White Americans

5% Other

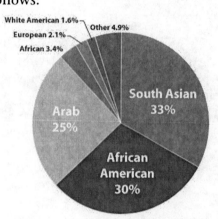

Council on American-Islam Relations
http://www.cair.com (accessed April 2014)

Growth of Islam in America

Immigration — It is the most important factor for this growth. At least 250,000 Muslims immigrate annually to the USA. Muslims come to the West seeking a better life for themselves and for their children.

Birth Rate — Because so many immigrants come from third world nations, their birth rates are much higher. It is not uncommon for Muslim families to have four or more children, more than twice the average number of children in most American families. Additionally, Muhammad encouraged his followers to spread Islam and increase the Muslim population by having many children (Sura 18:46).

Marriage — This takes pace between American non-Muslim women and Muslim men is the third factor. Quite often Muslim men come to America as students, on business or on tourist visas, with the intent to marry American women. More than ten thousand American non-Muslim women marry Muslim men each year and most of them will convert to Islam. This is part of the strategic plan to Islamize the West.

Conversion — Most statistics agree that about 250,000 Americans convert to Islam every year. The majority of converts are African American men who see traditional churches as unfriendly towards them and as out-dated institutions that fail to address their real needs. Other experts cite racism in America and in the church as a reason for the conversions. Researchers also believe that people are drawn to Islam because it requires its followers to follow strictly disciplined regimens such as praying five times a day and fasting.

Percentage of mosques in U.S. doing any of the following activities

Stress the importance of dawah (Muslim mission) to non-Muslims in the Mosque's teachings	92%
Visit a school or church to present Islam	71%
Write or call the media	70%
Write or call a political leader	61%
Participate in an interfaith dialogue or program	66%
Participate in an interfaith social service project	37%
Have a politician visit the mosque	41%
Any of the above	**96%**

Muslims tend to live in the bigger cities in the U.S. Currently the Muslim religious leaders are encouraging their people to move from the cities to the suburbs to further the spread of Islam in America.

Islam by the Numbers:

There are more than 2500 Mosques and Islamic centers in North America. It is estimated that each week one new Islamic center is being established.[3]

There are close to 200 Islamic schools, more than 450 Islamic associations, and 100 Islamic publications in North America today, most of which are funded by Saudi Arabia, Kuwait, and other oil producing Islamic nations.[4]

After reading these statistics you may feel overwhelmed and discouraged, but as Christians, we have to ask ourselves, "What can we do?" This subject is discussed in another lesson, but for now, keep these two sentences tucked in your memory:

1. Islam (the religion) is the criminal. Most Muslims (the followers of this religion) are the victims.

2. Muslims are not so much resistant to the Gospel as they are neglected by Christians.

Distribution of Muslim Centers in the U.S.
Research in Progress: 1855 Centers, October 2004

0
1-9
10-24
25-49
50-99
100+

---

[3]The Pluralism Project at Harvard University, Resources, http://www.pluralism.org/resources (accessed May 2014).

[4]Islam 101, History, http://www.islam101.com/history (accessed May 2014).

Answers from the Word of God

Side Trip: Check Out What the Bible Says

List some Christian denominations you are familiar with and find at least one belief or practice that you have in common with them.

Denomination	Common belief or practice

Are you able to relate to Christians from other denominations and work with them to further the kingdom of Christ? Read what Jesus prayed for in John 17:17-21.

Main Trip: A Missionary Heart

Bible Study Passage
Matthew 28:18-20

> "And Jesus came up and spoke to them, saying, 'All authority has been given to Me in heaven and on Earth. Go therefore and make disciples of all the nations, baptizing them in the name of the Father and the Son and the Holy Spirit, teaching them to observe all that I commanded you; and lo, I am with you always, even to the end of the age.'"

This passage from Matthew 28 is known as the Great Commission. It is Christ's command to His disciples to spread the gospel all over the world.

It is clear that Jesus' mission for His followers is to make His gospel known to all people through both words and deeds. We need to share the gospel with others and we need to reflect that gospel in our own daily lives.

Let's work our way through this passage so that we can understand what Jesus truly wants from us.

1. Why do we share the Gospel message?

Read Matthew 28:18 again. It is important to know that Jesus gives this command on the basis of His authority. This verse reminds us that Jesus is God Himself and all authority in heaven and on earth is His from the beginning of time. Our call to missions is based on the command from Jesus Christ, who is the Son of God and the only means of salvation.

2. Where do we share the Gospel?

In Matthew 28:19 Jesus commanded us to "Go therefore and make disciples of all the nations...." The commission to go to all nations is an expansion of Christ's earlier message to make it applicable to the Gentiles as well. When Jesus was in the flesh His ministry was focused on the disciples and the Jews. When Christ commissioned the disciples—and us—He commanded us to go into *all* the world.

Does this mean that we are all expected to train for overseas missions? No, while Christ certainly equips some to do this type of work, for many of us the mission of sharing the Gospel through word and deed will remain local. But in this age, even locally, we can reach the various different people groups who have come from all over the world to live among us. Our mission can include:

- Sharing in our neighborhood, our work, our school, and in our community.
- Building relationships that allow people to ask why our words and deeds are different from those of others.
- Living our lives deliberately in a way that reflects Jesus Christ.

3. How do we share the Gospel?

The method Christ commands us to use is discipleship. Read Matthew 28:20 again. At the heart of Christ's message the focus is always on relationships. The Great Commission is not a militant message to spread the Word through battles and hostility, but instead it is a message to share what we believe in order to reach people, to make them disciples, baptize them, and teach them the commandments of Jesus. We are not called to force others to make confessions of faith and then leave new believers to flounder on their own. We are called to invest our lives in new Christians in ways that lead them towards a life of faithfulness.

4. Who do we depend on?

The last portion of the great commission says "...lo, I am with you always, even to the end of the age." Jesus closes this commandment with an encouraging promise. He assures us that we will not take this trip on our own. He will be with us to the end of the age providing us with His wisdom, power,

DARE
TO EXPLORE

courage, strength, peace, joy, and mercy so that we can complete His Great Commission.

Taking Steps Towards Living Out the Great Commission

One key part to living this missions-centered life is the motivational part. While we all know that obedience requires us to be agents of the Great Commission, sometimes obedience is not motivation enough. We need to recognize and understand the great gift of salvation we have been given and know the message so well that we can't help but share it. Just as a great cook treasures practicing her skills with her family and friends, or a talented athlete seeks ways to use his gifts, so too should we look for ways to share our God-given gifts.

Perhaps you don't feel quite ready for a commitment to missions yet. Read what the Word of God says in Ephesians 2:10: "For we are His workmanship, created in Christ Jesus for good works, which God prepared beforehand so that we would walk in them."

We all have a role to play. You have one too, so seek Him and find the good works that He has prepared for you.

Private or Public

Do you keep your faith to yourself considering what you believe to be a private and personal matter? Many Christians are in daily contact with the same people for years without ever sharing their faith with them. Have you worked with someone for a long period of time without them knowing what you believe? Is there anyone in your sphere of influence who would be surprised to find out that you are a follower of Jesus? The call to make disciples is certainly not a call to offensively present your faith to others but it is a command to step out of your comfort zone in order to bring Christ to the world around you.

The majority of Muslims are proud of their religion and heritage to the extent that even though they may intend to spend the rest of their lives as U.S. citizens, they intentionally do not become westernized. In every aspect of their lives they make sure that their Islamic beliefs are evident to those around them. This extends well beyond regular mosque attendance. Many Muslims practice their faith in very public ways through public prayer five times a day, the wearing of headscarves as a sign of separateness, and shopping exclusively in *halal* markets. They also send their children to Arabic schools and Islamic center functions to reinforce their lifestyle and beliefs. A Muslim believer uses every opportunity to teach Westerners about Islam as a religion and culture,

believing that Islam is the true religion and that it is vital for everyone to hear the message and convert.

Be Zealous

Muslims believe so strongly that they have the truth, they are willing to risk ridicule, persecution, and even their lives for the sake of Islam. Where do you stand? Do you believe that the Bible is the absolute truth? Are you convinced that Christ is the only way to salvation? Are you willing to step out of your comfort zone to share that truth with others? Are you confident that the Holy Spirit will guide you through this process? Difficult as evangelism is, our Lord has promised us success. He said, "but you will receive power when the Holy Spirit has come upon you, and you shall be My witnesses... even to the remotest part of the earth" (Acts 1:8). This message was rephrased by the early missionary to India, A.J. Gordon, "It is not a matter of bringing the world to Christ; it is a matter of taking Christ to the world."[5] If we believe this we need to be zealous and courageous.

> How, then, can they call on the one they have not believed in? And how can they believe in the one of whom they have not heard? And how can they hear without someone preaching to them? And how can anyone preach unless they are sent? As it is written: "How beautiful are the feet of those who bring good news!" (Romans 10:14-15)

---

[5]Christy Wilson, *Self Supporting Witness Overseas*, Cassette. Deerfield InterVarsity, Urbana, 1973.

DARE
TO EXPLORE

Probing Deeper

1. Is there an Islamic center in your area? What do you know about it?

_____

_____

_____

_____

2. Share your feelings or experiences with regard to the spread of Islam where you live.

_____

_____

_____

_____

_____

3. Now that you have learned about the different sects of Islam, do you feel more equipped to understand news reports and your Muslim neighbors? Give an example.

_____

_____

_____

_____

_____

4. Have you taken the Great Commission to heart as a commandment, or is this an area you still have to address?

_____

_____

_____

_____

5. Think about the obstacles that keep you from sharing your faith. What practical steps can you take to begin to overcome them?

_____

_____

_____

_____

_____

Rest on the Road

Use this space to talk to God. Put in front of Him your fears and reservations. If there are particular people God is reminding you of, pray for God to prepare you to say the right things at the right time. Also pray that God will prepare their hearts to receive the Gospel message.

_____

_____

_____

_____

_____

_____

_____

_____

_____

_____

Points of Interest

Bible Passages

- The Book of Jonah (read this story of a reluctant missionary)
- Matthew 28:18-20, Mark 16:15, and Romans 10:14-16

Books

- Colson, Charles and Santilli Vaughn, Ellen. *Being The Body*. Thomas Nelson (2003)
- Mehmet, Ergun and Caner, Emir Fethi. *Unveiling Islam*. Kregel Publications (2009)

Web Sites

- Wilson, Christy. "Self Supporting Wittness Overseas." *Tentmaker Net*. http://www.tentmakernet.com/articles/selfsupporting.htm (accessed April 2014)
- Islam in America: The Pluralism Project at Harvard University. *Resources by Tradition*. http://www.pluralism.org/resources/tradition/?trad=9 (accessed April 2014)
- Gilchrist, John. "Muhammad and the Religion of Islam." *Answering Islam: A Christian-Muslim Dialog*. http://www.answering-islam.org/Gilchrist/Vol1/ (accessed April 2014)

Lesson 4

Janna or Heaven

Does It Matter What I Believe

Islam: Doctrine and Beliefs

Part I: The Five Main Muslim Beliefs

The basic doctrines of Islam are collectively known as the Five Doctrines of the Islamic Faith. They include belief in Allah, belief in angels, belief in the prophets, belief in the scriptures, and belief in the Final Judgment. In addition to these five beliefs, some texts include a sixth belief, that of Allah's divine decree and predestination. The Five Pillars or practices of Islam will be addressed in a different lesson.

1. The one god (Allah)

There is only one true god, whose name is Allah. He is numerically and absolutely one. Surrendering totally to Allah is required of every Muslim. (Allah is discussed in detail in lesson six.)

2. Spiritual Beings

Angels have no gender and are made of light, whereas humans are made of clay. All angels are considered good, except Iblis (Satan), who was sent out of heaven after he refused Allah's command to bow down to Adam. Although the angels work as messengers and helpers of Allah, none are considered to be superior to humans. The angels do not have free will and are completely obedient to Allah's commands. They have no ability to reason and therefore do not have the capacity, as humans do, to truly know Allah.

Muslims recognize another kind of supernatural creature, the Jinn, which can be differentiated from angels in several ways. Jinn, beings created from fire, are much lower than angels, are either male or female, have limited life spans, and can be virtuous or wicked. Like humans, they too receive revelations through Allah's prophets. Folk Islam is heavily loaded with the works of the Jinn in the lives of Muslims.

3. Prophets (Anbia)

Muslims believe that Allah has spoken through many prophets, such as Noah, Abraham, Moses, and Jesus. However, Muhammad was the last and most important in a long line of prophets who were entrusted with bringing scriptures to their peoples. According to Islam, the prophets are divided into two classes, "rasul" and "nabi." A rasul, or messenger, is a law-bringing prophet, given a major new revelation, and called to communicate what Allah sends to his people. A nabi, or prophet, is also one whom Allah speaks to, but his mission lies within the framework of an existing religion. According to Islam,

The Messengers According to Islam

1) Nuh (Noah)

2) Sahifat Ibrahim (Abraham)

3) Musa (Moses)

4) Isa (Jesus)

5) Muhammad

A famous Hadith says that the number of prophets is 124,000!

Hadith Ahmad bin Hanbal no. 21257

no prophet will come after Muhammad; therefore Allah sanctions Imams to guide the Muslims.

4. Holy Books (Al-Koutoub)

The Qur'an, meaning "recitation," is considered the holiest and final revelation of Allah. It is held to be the eternal, literal, word of Allah. Muslims believe that all scriptures are Allah's work, but that the people before the dawn of Islam had corrupted the original messages to suit their own inclinations. The Qur'an is considered the purest scripture on earth and free from tampering. It was revealed to Muhammad and preserved in the Arabic language. The other books believed by Muslims to have been given to the prophets by Allah are: scrolls given to Noah and Abraham (nothing is known about these texts), the first five books of the Old Testament; which they called Taurat, the Psalms, and the Injil (the Gospel). They claim that the Injil was corrupted and destroyed by the Christians because it tells of Muhammad's coming and it is not the same as the New Testament. Note that Muslims do not read these books, as they consider them ancient messages sent by Allah for a certain era or people group; only the Qur'an contains the everlasting message from Allah for the entire world.

5. The Final Judgment (Al-Dainouna)

Muslims believe there will be a final Day of Judgment. On that day Allah will weigh the good and the bad works on a scale. Janna (Heaven) is for the Muslims whose good works outweigh their bad deeds. The rest who did not do enough good will go to Al-Gehiem (Hell). Al-Gehiem is a place of endless pain, suffering, and torment. It is filled with flames, boiling water, and blistering wind. The time of the "Day of Judgment" is unknown to any but Allah. The angel Isafril will sound the trumpet and at that moment the order of the natural world will be inverted.

Anyone who denies these five basic tenets of Islam cannot be treated as a Muslim. Muslims believe that these doctrines are the basis of the divine religion and that every human is called by Allah to adopt these beliefs. A mu'min, (believer) who adopts these five beliefs and practices the "Pillars of Islam" might enjoy eternal paradise.

Part II: Additional Beliefs

Fatalism (Kissma)

Most Muslims follow a sixth doctrine, Kissma, which is a belief in Allah's divine decree and predestination. Only Allah ordains the fate of all mankind

---

The Books Sent by Allah

1) Sahifat Nuh
(scroll revealed to Noah)

2) Sahifat
(scroll revealed to Abraham)

3) Taurat
(book revealed to Moses)

4) Zabur
(Psalms revealed to David)

5) Injil
(Gospel revealed to Jesus)

6) Qur'an
(revealed to Muhammad)

which means that all people are predestined to spend eternity in either paradise or hell. This belief contradicts the fifth doctrine of Islam, which states that good works and belief in Allah and Muhammad lead to paradise. "Fatalism" is not the only contradiction in Islamic beliefs and teachings, but it poses one of the largest dilemmas for Muslim scholars.

The Muslim Paradise (Janna)

According to the Qur'an, paradise is a place for a Muslim to recline, eat, drink exquisite wines, and engage in physical pleasures with many beautiful women. There is no mention of any reward for women.

> "Surely the pious will be in Gardens and Bliss to them will be said: 'Eat and drink ye, with profit and health, because of your (good) deeds.' Reclining upon ranged settees. And We will marry them to wide-eyed huras. And We will supply them with fruits and flesh such as they crave for" (Sura 52:17, 19, 20).

Marriage

Muslims uphold marriage as an honorable religious command that every Muslim needs to undertake. Many Muslim groups consider marriage as "completing half of the religion," which means fulfilling half of one's religious obligation. Under Islamic law, a man is allowed to marry as many as four wives at one time and is encouraged to have as many children as possible in order to increase the 'Umma' of Islam.

Lying

Islam justifies lying in certain situations. There are several passages in the Qur'an and the Hadith which clearly state that unintentional lies are forgivable and that Muslims can gain pardon for even their *intentional* lies by performing extra duties, such as feeding and clothing the poor, or fasting for three days (Sura 5:89). Muslims can lie while under oath and can even falsely deny faith in Allah, as long as they maintain the profession of faith in their hearts (Sura 2:225 & 16:106).

In Hadith al-Ghazali, Vol. 3: pp.284–287, Muhammad emphasized the same concepts about lying: "One of Muhammad's daughters, Umm Kalthoum, testified that she had never heard the Apostle of Allah condone lying, except in these three situations: For reconciliation among people, in war, and amongst spouses, to keep peace in the family." For Muslims, according to these teachings, what they say and promise matters less than what they mean in their hearts!

Of course Islam has many more beliefs than those listed above. The other beliefs usually differ among the various sects of Islam. The ones presented here are the major doctrines that most Muslims agree upon.

Sin

In Islam sins are not all equal. Sometimes the same act can be good while at other times evil. For example adultery is forbidden. However, relationships with maidens and war captives are allowed. (Sura 33:52 and Sura 4:3). The Quran teaches that all people are sinful (Sura 96:6) but offers no solution or path to forgiveness outside of martyrdom.

Answers from the Word of God

Side Trip: Biblical Beliefs

Compare the five beliefs of Islam to those in the Christian faith. This will help you explain some of your own principles as a follower of Jesus to your Muslim friends.

Islamic Belief	Biblical Truth	Biblical Principle
Allah	John 1:1, 14, 18	
Angels	Colossians 2:18	
Prophets	Matthew 24:23, 24	
Holy Books	Revelation 22:18	
Paradise	I Thess. 4:13-18	

Main Trip: Heaven — The Ultimate Goal

Bible Study Passage
Luke 23:39-43

> "One of the criminals who were hanged there was hurling abuse at Him, saying, 'Are You not the Christ? Save Yourself and us!' But the other answered, and rebuking him said, 'Do you not even fear God, since you are under the same sentence of condemnation? And we indeed are suffering justly, for we are receiving what we deserve for our deeds; but this man has done nothing wrong.' And he was saying, 'Jesus, remember me when You come in Your kingdom!' And He said to him, 'Truly I say to you, today you shall be with Me in Paradise.'"

Eternal life, because it is so hard for humans to comprehend, is one of the major subjects addressed in the Word of God. People throughout the ages have tried to reach some kind of understanding as to what happens to us after death. All religions and cultures have offered various theories and beliefs as to the after-life, some emphasizing that works on earth determine your status after death and some asserting that nothing but luck determines the fate of a deceased human's soul. A number of belief systems even go to the extent of claiming that there is no life in any form or shape of any kind after death. Is

there truly life after death? Let's explore that.

Is There Life After Death?

Hundreds of books have been written to prove that there is life after death, but the Word of God is the best resource and it answers the question very clearly. Read what Jesus promises: "Truly, truly, I say to you, he who hears My word, and believes Him who sent Me, has eternal life, and does not come into judgment, but has passed out of death into life" (John 5:24). Jesus does not leave this important truth for humans to determine. He strongly and simply states that life after death does exist and no one should question it.

Jesus' Promise of Eternal Life

Jesus taught us that eternal life begins at the time of conversion and lasts forever. Eternal life could be spent in hell with Satan and his followers or in heaven with Jesus. Jesus told the thief on the cross that they would be together in paradise that same day. So whoever puts his trust in Jesus will have eternal life. Nothing else is required, neither works, nor rituals. God does not even require a minimum length of time as a believer to be assured of eternal life. The only thing the thief on the cross did was to put his trust in Christ; that is all God requires of us.

What a truly tremendous gift we have been given! Eternal life in heaven is not something awarded according to the merits of our actions, but is offered to us freely. The price was paid by Christ through His death on the cross and His victorious resurrection.

His Promise Will Never Change

God does not change and He keeps His promises; therefore, He will never change His mind about His love for us or His promise of eternal life.

His Word emphasizes this: "For I, the Lord, do not change; therefore you, O sons of Jacob, are not consumed" (Malachi 3:6) and "Jesus Christ is the same yesterday and today and forever" (Hebrews 13:8).

The Bible assures us repeatedly of God's continuous love for us: "The Lord appeared to us in the past, saying: 'I have loved you with an everlasting love; I have drawn you with loving-kindness'" (Jeremiah 31:3, NIV).

So, am I free to sin now that I know eternal life is guaranteed?

The assurance of eternal life does not mean that we have a free pass to sin without consequence. God calls us to live a holy life and He expects us to put all our physical and spiritual efforts towards achieving this goal. We need to remember that:

Read and Treasure These Assuring Promises of God

John 3:16
"For God so loved the world, that He gave His only begotten Son, whoever believes in Him shall not perish, but have eternal life."

John 3:36
"He who believes in the Son has eternal life; but he who does not obey the Son will not see life, but the wrath of God abides on him."

I John 5:13
"These things I have written to you who believe in the name of the Son of God, so that you may know that you have eternal life."

1. Not only does Christ save us from the wages of sin (death), but He also sets us free from the power of sin. "So if the Son sets you free, you will be free indeed" (John 8:36).

2. What God did for us on the cross compels us to obedience. If we love someone we long to please them and we try not to intentionally offend or anger them. This same mindset applies to our relationship with God, but the scale is so much greater. God loved us first and our response to the great continuous gift of that love can only be obedience.

> "What then? Shall we sin because we are not under law but under grace? May it never be! Do you not know that when you present yourselves to someone as slaves for obedience, you are slaves of the one whom you obey, either of sin resulting in death, or of obedience resulting in righteousness? But thanks be to God that though you were slaves of sin, you became obedient from the heart to that form of teaching to which you were committed, and having been freed from sin, you became slaves of righteousness" (Romans 6:15-18).

However, there will be times when the flesh sins, but for such times the Bible says "If we confess our sins, He is faithful and righteous to forgive us our sins and to cleanse us from all unrighteousness" (I John 1:9).

What Will Heaven Look Like?

The Bible reveals very few definite details about what heaven will look like, what the afterlife will feel like, and what exactly happens when we die. Our finite minds could never comprehend the realities of heaven and God chooses not to burden us with information we can't understand. But there are a few glimpses that God gives us through His Word to help us look forward to our heavenly home:

- *Heaven will be a place with no pain and tears.* Read what the Bible says about how God will care for us in heaven. "And I heard a loud voice from the throne, saying, 'Behold, the tabernacle of God is among men, and He will dwell among them, and they shall be His people, and God Himself will be among them and He will wipe away every tear from their eyes; and there will no longer be any death; there will no longer be any mourning, or crying, or pain; the first things have passed away'" (Revelation 21:3-4).

- *Heaven will have beauty beyond our imagination.* "The wall was made of jasper, and the city of pure gold, as pure as glass. The foundations of the city walls were decorated with every kind of precious stone... The twelve gates were twelve pearls, each gate made of a single pearl. The great street of the city was of pure gold, like transparent glass... The city does not need

the sun or the moon to shine on it, for the glory of God gives it light, and the Lamb is its lamp. The nations will walk by its light, and the kings of the earth will bring their splendor into it. On no day will its gates ever be shut, for there will be no night there. The glory and honor of the nations will be brought into it. Nothing impure will ever enter it, nor will anyone who does what is shameful or deceitful, but only those whose names are written in the Lamb's book of life" (Revelation 21:18-27, NIV).

- *Heaven will be a place where we can worship God in the perfection and glory He deserves.* "Who will not fear, O Lord, and glorify Your name? For You alone are holy; For all The nations will come and worship before You, for Your righteous acts have been revealed" (Revelation 15:4).

Eternal life is God's promise to all who put their trust in Christ. Heaven is a reality and it will be our eternal home. What is your response to that promise?

"After this I looked, and there before me was a great multitude that no one could count, from every nation, tribe, people and language, standing before the throne and before the Lamb. They were wearing white robes and were holding palm branches in their hands. And they cried out in a loud voice: 'Salvation belongs to our God, who sits on the throne, and to the Lamb.'" (Revelation 7:9-10)

Probing Deeper

1. Use your imagination to describe what heaven will look like.

_____

_____

_____

_____

2. How do the Muslim beliefs about paradise differ from the Christian beliefs about heaven?

_____

_____

_____

_____

_____

3. According to our Bible passage Luke 23:39-43 (the thief on the cross), how does someone get to heaven?

_____

_____

_____

_____

4. At what time in your life did the meaning of the death of Christ and His resurrection begin to make sense to you?

_____

_____

_____

_____

5. On a scale from one to ten, how certain are you of your own eternal life with Jesus? (One being completely doubtful and ten being totally assured.)

_____

_____

_____

_____

_____

Rest on the Road

Use this space to talk to God. If you are not completely sure that you will spend eternity with Jesus Christ, now is the time to do what the thief on the cross did. If you are completely certain, fill these lines with praises for God's unchanging promise.

_____

_____

_____

_____

_____

_____

_____

_____

_____

_____

_____

Points of Interest

Bible Passages

- Luke 23:29-43
- I Thessalonians 4:13-18
- Revelation 21
- Matthew 22:23-31

Books

- Ricker, Robert S. *Assured of Heaven.* Assurance Books (2009)
- Geisler, Norman L. and Saleeb, Abdul. *Answering Islam.* Baker Books (2003)

Web Sites

- Thompson, Keith. "Heaven vs. Jannah: Assessing the Dilemma." *Answering Islam: A Christian-Muslim Dialog.* www.answering-islam.org/authors/thompson/paradise.html (accessed April 2014)
- About.com. Islam. http://islam.about.com/od/basicbeliefs (accessed April 2014)

Lesson 5

Good Works

Can We Do Enough Good to be Saved?

The Islamic Practices

Part I: The Five Pillars of Islam

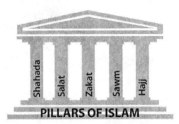

The Five Pillars are the framework for the Muslim's life and discipline. Successful adherence to the pillars satisfies the will of Allah. These principles, along with the five Muslim beliefs which we discussed previously, form the basis for the Muslim's hope to enter Janna.

Pillar 1—*Shahada* (The Confession of the Creed)

The creed of Islam is fully declared in this one statement in Arabic: "Ash-hadu anna la ilaha illa Allah, wa ash-hadu anna Muhammad rasulu Allah." It means, "I testify there is no god but Allah, and Muhammad is the messenger of Allah." Sincerity in the tone of voice while saying the confession is necessary for it to be valid. It must be uttered in Arabic and then translated into the speaker's own language to be understood. The Shahada must be honored until death, denial of it nullifies any hope to enter Janna. A Muslim will repeat the Shahada thousands of times in prayer and in everyday conversation during his or her lifetime, believing that its utterance brings great rewards.

Pillar 2—*Salat* (Prayer)

Prayer is practiced five times a day: before sunrise, at noon, in mid-afternoon, at sunset, and in the evening. The noon Friday prayer in the mosque is the most important of all and attending it is mandatory for adult males, who must practice it in ritual purity. Prayers in the mosques are led by respected lay leaders and Imams. Women are encouraged to pray in their homes and are taught that praying in their homes is of more value than in the mosques.

Each prayer is preceded by a ceremonial washing of the face, mouth, nose, ears, hands, and feet. While praying the Muslim is required to face Mecca, kneeling on a small rug used only for this purpose. The prayers consist of specific sentences recited from the Qur'an. The whole ritual is a strictly prescribed set of postures, bending, and prostrations that differ slightly between the orthodox schools. Arabic is the only language Muslims are allowed to use while praying even if they do not speak it or understand it. In Islam, prayer is an expression of submission to Allah and not a connection or a relationship.

If a Muslim has a request of Allah, it is not called prayer (Salat) but Du-aa, which means supplication. There are certain times when Du-aa is more likely

The Shahada

is compared to the sinner's prayer or baptism. It is the sign of converting to Islam. Once uttered, a person cannot renounce Islam without the penalty of death.

Arabic prayer tutorials

There are websites devoted to teaching non-Arabic speakers how to say prayers with proper preparation, posture, and phonetics.

to be accepted by Allah, such as late at night, after the crowing of a rooster, during Ramadan, or at the beginning of war.[1]

Pillar 3—*Zakat* (Alms-giving)

Muslims who have surplus money at the end of the year, after paying for their own basic needs, must pay a certain percentage to help others. This almsgiving is called Zakat, from the Arabic word which means both "to purify" and "to grow." Muslims believe that giving to others purifies their own wealth, increases its value, and reminds them that everything they have is a trust from Allah. Paying Zakat is required of every adult Muslim man or woman who possesses wealth of a certain minimum amount. It is usually given to the mosque leader who is responsible for giving it to the poor.

How Much to Pay in Zakat: The amount of money paid in Zakat depends on the amount and type of wealth one possesses, but is usually considered to be a minimum of 2.5 percent of a person's "extra" wealth. Because the specific calculations of Zakat are rather detailed and dependent on individual circumstances, Zakat calculators have been developed to assist with the process.

Sadaqah: In addition to the required alms, Muslims are encouraged to give in charity at all times according to their means. Voluntary charity is called sadaqah, from the Arabic word meaning "truth" and "honesty." Sadaqah may be given at any time and in any amount.

Pillar 4—*Sawm* (Fasting)

In Islam fasting is a public event, not a private one. Muslims abstain from food and drink, as well as smoking and intimacy, between sunrise and sunset during the month of *Ramadan*, the ninth month in the Muslim calendar. After sunset, feasting and other celebrations take place among families and in the communities. The Ramadan fast starts at dawn, defined as the moment when the human eye can distinguish a white thread from a black one, and ends at dusk, when the eye is again no longer able to distinguish the difference. The end of the month of Ramadan is always marked by a feast, known as *Id al-Fitr*, or break-fast feast. Ramadan was the month during which Muhammad had his first encounter with the spirit in Cave Hira. Muslims try to read and recite the entire Qur'an during this month.

Pillar 5—*Hajj* (Pilgrimage)

All Muslims, men and women who are economically and physically able, are required to journey as pilgrims to Mecca at least once in their lifetime. No non-Muslim is allowed to visit Mecca or witness the Hajj. The season begins

The Muslim Lunar Months

To distinguish themselves from the Jews, Christians, and pagan Arabs, Muslims measure their year by the cycles of the moon rather than the sun, so the Muslim lunar year is eleven days shorter than the Christian solar year. Muslims are forbidden to adjust their year by adding an extra month as the Jews do to keep their lunar calendar in sync with the seasons. Hence, the months of the Muslim year do not relate to the seasons.

[1]Islam Awareness, *Dawah*, http://www.islamawareness.net (accessed April 2014).

in the tenth month, the month following Ramadan, and lasts through the middle of the twelfth month. Muslims associate the origin of the Hajj and the founding of the *Ka'aba* with Abraham, who was believed to have built the Ka'aba.[2]

According to the Hadith Bukhari (Volume 2, Book 26, No. 596), the Muslim pilgrim "shall return (from Mecca) as pure from sin as the day on which he was born." And "The reward of a pilgrim is paradise." The completion of this practice gives the Muslim both a satisfying feeling and a respected status in his or her community. The pilgrim is honored by the new title "Al-hajj" for a man and "Al-hajja" for a woman.

Part II: Jihad, the Unwritten Sixth Pillar

Some Muslim groups regard jihad as the unwritten sixth pillar of Islam.[3]

Muslims in the west claim that *jihad* does not mean holy war. In Arabic, the word jihad literally means "struggle" or "strife." It is true that part of the jihad is the personal strife to please Allah in prayers, fasting, and good deeds, but the widely accepted worldwide use of jihad among Muslims is to describe the religious war waged against the non-Muslims. Jihad is a current religious duty, established in the Qur'an and in the Hadith as a divine institution. It is used specifically for the purpose of advancing Islam.

Perhaps the one Qur'anic verse that wholly summarizes the call to jihad is found in Sura 9:29. This verse is called the verse of the sword:

> *"and fight those who acknowledge not the Religion of Truth [i.e. Islam], from among the People of the Book (i.e. Christians & Jews), until they pay the Jizya tax with willing submission, and feel themselves subdued."*

Throughout history, when an infidel's country was conquered by a Muslim ruler, its inhabitants were offered three alternatives:

1. **Converting to Islam**, in which case the conquered people submit to the Muslim state.

2. **Paying a poll-tax (Jizya)**, as a penalty for those who want to keep their own faith and not embrace Islam. It has been recorded that in some places the tax reached 90% of the family's gross annual income.

---

[2]Norman Geisler, Answering Islam: *The Crescent In Light Of The Cross* (Grand Rapids: Baker Books, 2002) 98.

[3]Norman Geisler, Answering Islam, 178.

3. **Death by the sword,** to those who will neither pay the Jizya nor convert to Islam.

The duty of religious war (which all commentators agree is a duty extending to all time) is laid down in the Qur'an in hundreds of verses. Remarkably, all those verses were given to Muhammad in the Medina period, after he had established himself as a paramount ruler and was in a position to dictate terms to his enemies. All Muslims are ordered to participate in jihad or support it and those who do not are considered infidels. Here are some of the verses confirming jihad as religious war: Sura 25:52; 2:193 and 216; 2:214–215; 8:39–42

Muslims practice the five pillars and jihad in the hope of gaining favor with Allah and going to Janna. They work tirelessly and zealously to please their god, but there is no assurance of a physical or eternal reward for them no matter how hard they work. Ultimately, Muslims can never be sure of their eternal destiny except if they die in jihad.

Special Rewards for Muslims Who Die in Jihad (Martyrs)[4]

1. No Punishment

2. Forgiveness of Sin

3. Security from Judgment

4. Seventy-two Virgins in Paradise

5. Rewards for Relatives

---

[4] John Ankerberg, *The Truth About Islam & Jihad,* (Eugene, Harvest House, 2009) 28.

Answers from the Word of God

Side Trip: Doing or Being

Now that you have read what Muslims must practice in order to please their god, compare the pillars of Islam with what Jesus taught about these same subjects long before Islam was established. Remember that in Christianity we obey Jesus' teachings out of love, not out of fear of condemnation.

Muslim Pillars	Bible Passage	Jesus' Teaching
Prayer	Matthew 6:5-15	
Fasting	Matthew 6:16-18	
Alms Giving	Matthew 6:1-2	
Pilgrimage	John 4:19-24	
Jihad	Matthew 5:43-44	

Main Trip: Faith and Works in the Bible

Bible Study Passage
James 2:14-26

"What use is it, my brethren, if someone says he has faith but he has no works? Can that faith save him? If a brother or sister is without clothing and in need of daily food, and one of you says to them, 'Go in peace, be warmed and be filled,' and yet you do not give them what is necessary for their body, what use is that? Even so faith, if it has no works, is dead, being by itself. But someone may well say, 'You have faith and I have works; show me your faith without the works, and I will show you my faith by my works.' You believe that God is one You do well; the demons also believe, and shudder. But are you willing to recognize, you foolish fellow, that faith without works is useless? Was not Abraham our father justified by works when he offered up Isaac his son on the altar? You see that faith was working with his works, and as a result of the works, faith was perfected; and the Scripture was fulfilled which says, 'And Abraham believed God, and it was reckoned to him as righteousness' and he was called the friend of God. You see that a man is justified by works and not by faith alone. In the same way, was not Rahab the harlot also justified by

works when she received the messengers and sent them out by another way? For just as the body without the spirit is dead, so also faith without works is dead."

Throughout history, people have approached the question of faith versus works in many different ways, as evidenced by the wide variety of religions and denominations currently in practice all over the world. That is why the Word of God addresses this subject deeply and clearly. One well-known passage is the one you have just read and the other is Ephesians 2:8-10. Let's look at what these passages say and find out what God teaches us through them about faith and works.

Works in the Word of God

God inspired James through the Holy Spirit to address the inseparable link between faith and works in chapter 2:14–26. Through a series of questions and answers James points out that works which are pleasing to God are part of the very nature of the Christian faith. James even goes so far as to say that faith without works is dead. The powerful image that James uses is his example of a brother in need; who among us would offer only words of encouragement to a person in need of food and drink? If someone needs a glass of water we give it to him, not to earn our way to heaven, but because it is the right thing to do. In this situation, our faith is shown by our works, not by words. Not that words are unimportant, or that there will not be times when words are all that we can offer, but the real test of our words is whether or not we have the actions to back them up. Notice that in both the Old and the New Testaments, God expects His people to obey Him through both words and deeds. For example, Isaiah urged the people of Israel to put meaning into their religious rituals by sharing bread with the hungry and covering the naked (Isaiah 58:7–9). In the New Testament, Jesus confirmed this teaching by promising the kingdom to those who feed and clothe the "least of these my brethren" (Matthew 25:31–46).

Works Do Not Save

The question that might arise when you read the above passage from James 2 is: Are we encouraged to go out and do good works to earn our salvation? The answer is decidedly, no, of course not. Remember that Abraham's journey started with his faith and obedience to God; his actions or works came as a natural result of that faith. Abraham's obedience through faith went so far as to be willing to offer his own son as a sacrifice when God asked it of him. Martin Luther describes the Christian life in this way: "O it is a living, busy, active mighty thing, this faith. It is impossible for it not to be doing good

things incessantly." [5]Does your relationship to Jesus Christ compel you to do good works for His glory? Is your faith dormant or alive? "For just as the body without the spirit is dead, so also faith without works is dead" (James 2:26).

Salvation: The Gift of God

So if works are the wrong way to reconcile with God, then what is the correct way according to the Bible? Read what God tells us in Ephesians 2:8–10:

> "For by grace you have been saved through faith; and that not of your-selves, it is the gift of God; not as a result of works, so that no one may boast. For we are His workmanship, created in Christ Jesus for good works, which God prepared beforehand so that we would walk in them."

Salvation, then, is the gift of God to us! We can never earn salvation by our works. Salvation is given by the grace of God and received through faith alone, not just any faith, but faith according to the Word of God; that God the Father sent His only Son to pay the price for our sins and whoever puts his faith in Jesus Christ will be saved.

> "Jesus said to him, 'I am the way, and the truth, and the life; no one comes to the Father but through Me'" (John 14:6)

When we realize that faith is not man's gift to God, but rather that salvation is God's gift to man through Jesus Christ, then it becomes clear that salvation is not something that we can gain or lose by our works. There is no miracle formula or ritual. Saying the right words, praying the appropriate number of prayers at the right time of day, or even spending most of our days doing good works, could never earn us our way into God's presence. We are by nature depraved sinners, and if the promise of salvation were as shaky as to be dependent on our works, we would all surely be doomed to hell. Only the grace of God that comes into our lives through faith in Jesus Christ can renew us from the inside and reconcile us with God. He offers you this gift with no strings attached; it is free, priceless, and eternal.

Contradictions?

Does James chapter two contradict Ephesians chapter two? Let's explore this together briefly. Paul, writing to the Ephesians, emphasizes that faith is not "of yourself," it is the gift of God, but he also states that the journey of faith does not stop at conversion. Rather, it continues to grow and regenerate when we obediently start doing the good works that Jesus has prepared for us to do. In other words, anyone who is a true follower of Christ will, by his new

---

[5]Martin Luther, *Commentary on Romans*, Trans. J. Theodore Mueller (Grand Rapids: Zondervan, 1954), xvii.

nature, demonstrate his or her faith through good works. James reiterates that in his writings, making it clear that true faith will, by its very nature, produce good works: "You have faith and I have works; show me your faith without the works, and I will show you my faith by my works."

In conclusion, faith and works are both part of the Christian life. Faith is the free gift of God through grace and works are our natural response to that gift. Such a great gift must arouse a great response. Do you feel compelled by your faith to have your every action reflect Jesus' active presence in your life?

"Whether, then, you eat or drink or whatever you do, do all to the glory of God." (I Corinthians 10:31)

Probing Deeper

1. Are you primarily a doer or a thinker? How does this impact your spiritual life?

_____

_____

_____

_____

_____

2. From what you have learned about how Muslims pray, list some reasons why this way cannot be from the true God.

_____

_____

_____

_____

_____

3. For a Muslim, dying as a martyr in jihad is the only way to guarantee paradise. How does this make you feel towards Muslims?

_____

_____

_____

_____

_____

4. List some good works you do out of obligation or fear rather than love.

_____

_____

_____

_____

_____

DARE
TO EXPLORE

5. Search the areas in your life where changes need to be made, in order to reflect your faith in Jesus in a more clear way.

_____

_____

_____

_____

_____

Rest on the Road

Use this space to talk to God about the changes he has inspired you to make in your course of action regarding good works.

_____

_____

_____

_____

_____

_____

_____

_____

_____

_____

_____

Points of Interest

Bible Passages

- Genesis 22 (Abraham offers his son Isaac)

- Joshua 2 and 6 (The story of Rahab)

- James 2 and Ephesians 2

Books

- Swindoll, Charles R. *The Grace Awakening.* Thomas Nelson (1996)

- Kaltner, John. *Islam: What Non-Muslims Should Know.* Augsburg. Fortress Publishers (2003)

Web Sites

- Bingham, Geoffrey. "The Matter of the Muslim and Islam." *Answering Islam: A Christian-Muslim Dialog.* www.answering-islam.org/Intro/islam_1.pdf (accessed April 2014)

- Hartwig, Mark. "Spread by the Sword?" *Answering Islam: A Christian-Muslim Dialog.* http://www.answering-islam.org/Terrorism/by_the_sword.html (accessed April 2014)

- Islam Awareness. *Dawah.* http://www.islamawareness.net (accessed April 2014)

- Shamoun, Sam. "A Million Dollars for 'Holy War' Our Counter Challenge to Jamal Badawi." *Answering Islam: A Christian-Muslim Dialog* http://www.answering-islam.org/Shamoun/badawi_holy_war.htm (accessed April 2014)

- Shamoun, Sam. "Kill Them Wherever You Find Them Addressing the Lies and Distortions of One Muslim Dawagandist" *Answering Islam: A Christian-Muslim Dialog* http://www.answering-islam.org/Responses/Abualrub/jihad.htm (accessed April 2014)

- Bailey, Richard P. "Jihad The Teaching of Islam From Its Primary Sources—The Quran and Hadith." *Answering Islam: A Christian-Muslim Dialog* http://www.answering-islam.org/Bailey/jihad.html (accessed April 2014)

Lesson 6

The LORD God or Allah

The God of The Bible is Like No Other God

Islam: Allah, the God of Muslims

Islam is a religion that stands against the triune God of the Bible: God the Father, God the Son, and God the Holy Spirit. The God of Islam is not The LORD God but Allah. Let's explore how Allah became the god of Islam.

Part I: The Origin of Allah[1]

The Moon God with the crescent on his chest

Allah's Name: Allah was the title given to the moon-god "Sin" in the Arabian Peninsula even before Muhammad's time. This pagan god was "Al-ilah," the chief god. Eventually the title was shortened to the name Allah. When the popularity of the moon-god faded for many pagan groups, the Arab tribes near Mecca still considered him the greatest of the 360 gods at the Ka'bah. Mecca grew to be a shrine for this ancient god. To please him, pagan Arabs often gave their children names that contained his name, Allah. Muhammad's own father was named Abdullah, which means the servant of Allah.

Muhammad's use of "Allah" no longer had the implication of a generic title for the chief god. He redefined it to become the personal name of the one god of Islam. In other words, the pagan god "Sin" was "Al-ilah Sin," but Muhammad used the title "Al-ilah" or its shortened version "Allah" as a proper name for his god.

Allah's history: Islam claims "Allah" to be the same proper name used in the Bible for God. The Qur'an teaches that Allah revealed himself to the patriarchs of the Bible, as well as to the prophets, such as Moses and Isa, and finally to Muhammad. Since Allah's revelation to Muhammad is the final one, superceding Judaism and Christianity, the logical next step is that Islam now should be the only faith for everyone. The Quran teaches that we should all become Muslims! The flaw in this argument is that the God of the Bible who revealed His message is "Yahweh" not "Allah." His name is different, His nature is different, and as you will see later in this chapter, His attributes are very different.

Muhammad's god: Muhammad took the concept of the Moon-god, Allah, and repackaged him to become the one god of the Muslim religion. He combined Allah with the Jewish and Christian God in order to draw more followers. This is the reason why Muslims truly believe Allah to be the God of Abraham. Muhammad went to the extent of facing Jerusalem while praying

[1]Sam Shamoun, *"Allah of Islam, Is He Yahweh God of the Bible?"* http://answeringislam.org/Responses/Abualrub/allahs_identity.htm (accessed August 2014).

66

DARE TO EXPLORE

at the beginning of his call, and claimed that God sent him to the Jews as a prophet. However, when the Jews ridiculed him and refused to accept him as a valid prophet, Muhammad waged wars against them. After this failure, Muhammed began praying facing Mecca, the shrine of his idol god Allah. To this day, Muslims still face Mecca when they pray. Muham-mad later made Mecca the pilgrimage city of Islam.

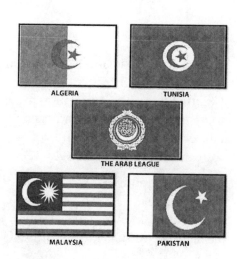

ALGERIA TUNISIA

THE ARAB LEAGUE

MALAYSIA PAKISTAN

The Flags of Islamic Nations

The use of the crescent moon as the symbol for Islam, which is placed on the flags of Islamic nations and on the top of mosques and minarets, is a throwback to the days when Allah was worshiped as the Moon-god in Mecca.

Part II: Allah's Attributes

Muhammad said in one Hadith: "To God belongs 99 names, 100 minus 1, anyone who memorizes them will enter Paradise; He (God) is odd (i.e., he is the Only One), and He loves odd numbers." Most Muslim scholars agree that Allah has many more names, but the 99 names (or attributes) mentioned in this quote are the primary and most important names of Allah. Which names exactly are included in the 99 varies according to different Islamic groups. Most of these attributes are similar to those of the biblical God, which is one of the reasons why Muslims claim that we all worship the same God. When faced with this argument by a member of the Muslim community, try to focus on presenting the biblical principles concerning who our God truly is. One of the best ways to do this is to guide them towards the following facts about the God of the Bible that contradict the attributes of Allah in the Qur'an. By doing this, Muslims will be able to make a comparison and face some truths about Allah. An important reminder: always share information in a loving and non-threatening way, truly trying to exemplify the compassion Jesus showed when He himself interacted with non-believers.

Some Positive Attributes of Allah

Al-Qadim: Allah is eternal. He has neither a beginning nor an end.

Al-Qadir: Allah is omnipotent. He has power over all things.

Al-Alim: Allah is omniscient. He is all-knowing.

Al-Hai: Allah is living. He is alive and will remain alive forever

Al-Mudrik: Allah is omnipresent. He is all-hearing, all-seeing.

The LORD God	Allah
GOD is love: "For God so loved the world…" (John 3:16). "How often I wanted to gather your children together, the way a hen gathers her chicks under her wings, and you were unwilling" (Matthew 23:37).	**Allah is *wadud:*** love is merely an expression of approval and acts of kindness to those who do good. "…Lo! Allah loveth the beneficent" (Sura 2:195). Allah is above the feeling of love.
GOD is all goodness: "Let no one say when he is tempted, 'I am being tempted by God;' for God cannot be tempted by evil, and He Himself does not tempt anyone" (James 1:13).	**Allah is the source of evil:** "And (the unbelievers) *schemed* and planned, and Allah schemed also, and the best of schemers is Allah" (Sura 3:54). Allah is macker, deceiver, the one who misleads.
GOD's message does not change: "Forever O Lord your Word is settled in heaven" (Psalm 119:89). "…the Word of the Lord endures forever…" (1 Peter 1:25).	**Allah changes his message:** "None of Our revelations do We abrogate or cause to be forgotten but *We substitute something better or similar…*" (Sura 2:106).
GOD is all knowing: "O Lord, You have searched me and known me" (Psalm 139:1). "He counts the number of the stars; He gives names to all of them. Great is our Lord and abundant in strength; His understanding is infinite" (Psalm 147:4-5).	**Allah makes scientific and historical mistakes:** "Until, when he reached the setting of the sun, he found it set in a spring of murky water (muddy spring)…" (Sura 18:86). "Mary! O sister of Aaron!" (Sura 19:27-28). Allah is addressing Mary the mother of Jesus, though there is 1400 years difference between the two women.
GOD is our heavenly Father: "For if you forgive others for their transgressions, your heavenly Father will also forgive you" (Matthew 6:14).	**Allah is the master:** He always addresses Muslims as "slaves" in the Qur'an. "Say: O My slaves who have been prodigal to their own hurt! Despair not of the mercy of Allah, Who forgiveth all sins. Lo! He is the Forgiving, the Merciful" (Sura 39:53).

In conclusion, we can definitely determine that the god of Islam is not the same God that Christians worship. He is not a father but a master, accepting only those who submit to him with unquestioning obedience. The fact that Islam's god is unable to love his creation, in the way that a truly magnificent creator should love the works of his hands, reveals that he is not the creator. It is a pity that millions of people worship this god out of fear instead of worshiping the true God out of love, and what a huge ministry opportunity this presents to Christians who are willing to share the truth about our loving God.

Answers from the Word of God

Side Trip: The Names of God

Let's look at some of the names God uses in the Bible to describe Himself. Meditate on these names while you pray. This will bring a new depth and understanding to the Mighty God whom you worship and serve.

Title of God	Bible Passage	Your Reflections
I Am	Exodus 3:13-15 John 8:58	
Shepherd	Isaiah 40:11 John 10:11-14	
Alpha and Omega	Revelation 1:8 Revelation 21:6	
Yahweh Jireh	Genesis 22:14 Psalm 83:18	
Everlasting Father	Isaiah 9:6 Matthew 6:8-10	

Main Trip: God, Our Heavenly Father

Bible Study Passage
Read Luke 15:11-32.

The story of the Prodigal Son is one of Jesus' most well-known parables. The story is relatively simple, but it communicates a vital message about the nature of God. The younger of two sons in a family is sinful and disobedient to his father, rebelling against everything the father has taught him. This son demands his share of the inheritance before his father's death and leaves his family to engage in physically, emotionally, and spiritually destructive behavior. The prodigal son's father has every right to totally forget his reckless son and to cut him off from further contact with the family, but he does not. This father, who is a reflection of our Heavenly Father, waits eagerly for his son's return. As he sees him coming from afar, he runs and falls on his neck and kisses him. The father accepts him lovingly, forgives him, and makes a feast in his honor to welcome him back as a true son. This is how God acts when

we wander away, and this is how He welcomes us back when we return in repentance.

Jesus Christ uses this beautiful parable to reveal to His disciples and to us several of God's characteristics: His Love, Mercy, Grace, and most of all His Fatherly Heart. In other lessons we have explored God's unconditional and immutable love for us, as well as the undeserved mercy and grace He bestows on His people. In this lesson let's focus on the unique relationship we have with our Creator as our Heavenly Father.

God's Fatherhood

One of the most unique features of the Christian faith is that according to the Bible we can call God our "Father." Therefore, if God calls Himself the Father of His people, this must mean that He is willing to enter into a deep personal relationship with us. As John explains it: "See how great a love the Father has bestowed on us, that we would be called children of God; and such we are" (I John 3:1).

"We are all children of God" is a commonly used phrase in the world today, but in truth and according to the Bible, we are all God's creation. Only those who have a relationship with Jesus are children of God. To be children of God is a designation that sets us apart from creation because it includes a two-way, personal relationship with God. This can only take place when we become a new creation in Christ; "Therefore if anyone is in Christ, he is a new creature; the old things passed away; behold, new things have come" (II Corinthians 5:17).

How does this happen?

God adopts us into His family at the moment we turn from our old sinful ways and choose to follow Christ our Savior and Redeemer; at that very moment a new nature is created in us and we become His adopted children.

> "Yet to all who received him, to those who believed in His name, He gave the right to become children of God" (John 1:12, NIV).

> "For you have not received a spirit of slavery leading to fear again, but you have received a spirit of adoption as sons by which we cry out, 'Abba! Father!'" (Romans 8:15).

What happens when we are adopted into God's family?

- We receive a new name—Children of God. (John 1:12)
- All the promises of the Word of God become ours. (II Peter 1:3–4)
- We acquire the longing to live Holy lives. (Ephesians 1:4-5)

71

- We become ambassadors for Christ. (II Corinthians 5:19–21)
- We become heirs to the Kingdom of God. (Titus 3:7)

This amazing gift, becoming Children of God, gives us a freedom like never before. We are liberated from the power of sin as well as from the bondage of our old nature. As Peter says, "For by these He has granted to us His precious and magnificent promises, so that by them you may become partakers of the divine nature, having escaped the corruption that is in the world by lust" (II Peter 1:4).

Our Father

What a wonderful privilege it is to call God our "Father." We can enter into His presence fully knowing that we belong to Him and that we reached home. Jesus taught us to address our prayers to "Our Father who art in Heaven." When we are adopted into God's family we can boldly call Him "Abba, Father."

Because of our fallen nature, fatherhood has been sadly distorted. Some of us grew up without a father figure in our lives; others had to live with cruel, abusive, detached, or careless fathers. As a result of these experiences we have developed a false sense of fatherhood. Due to this faulty perception, it can be difficult to understand God's perfect love for us as our father. However, the good news is that He promises to fill that void and restore a right understanding of fatherhood if we allow Him to work in us through His Holy Spirit. "A father of the fatherless and a judge for the widows is God in His holy habitation. God makes a home for the lonely; He leads out the prisoners into prosperity" (Psalm 68:5-6).

God the perfect Father

A good father provides for, comforts, protects, disciplines, and loves us; God is the perfect Father to us.

God provides for even the most basic of our needs. In the Sermon on the Mount, Jesus reminds us: "Look at the birds of the air, that they do not sow, nor reap nor gather into barns, and yet your heavenly Father feeds them. Are you not worth much more than they?" (Matthew 6:26).

In times of trouble, we can run to Him for comfort and protection. God is the ultimate comforter: "You are my hiding place; You preserve me from trouble; You surround me with songs of deliverance" (Psalm 32:7). "When my anxious thoughts multiply within me, your consolations delight my soul" (Psalm 94:19).

Just as an earthly father is there to instruct, correct, and even discipline us when we stray, so is our Heavenly Father. "My son, do not reject the discipline of the Lord or loathe His reproof, for whom the Lord loves He reproves, even as a father corrects the son in whom he delights" (Proverbs 3:11–12).

God the Father loves us with an eternal love. "I have loved you with an everlasting love" (Jeremiah 31:3). As flawed, fallen human beings, we cannot fathom this type of love, but thankfully we can accept it gratefully from our Father!

These truths about God our Father should fill us with great hope for eternal life and spur us to live as people who reflect God's love in the best ways we can in this life. We long for the day when we will be like Him and see Him just as He is.

> "See how great a love the Father has bestowed on us, that we would be called children of God; and such we are. For this reason the world does not know us, because it did not know Him. Beloved, now we are children of God, and it has not appeared as yet what we will be. We know that when He appears, we will be like Him, because we will see Him just as He is. And everyone who has this hope fixed on Him purifies himself, just as He is pure" (I John 3:1–3).

Probing Deeper

1. Share some nicknames you know for "father" in English or other languages.

_____

_____

_____

_____

_____

2. What are two key characteristics about Allah that you cannot accept in a god?

_____

_____

_____

_____

_____

3. What are the characteristics missing in the Allah of Islam that exist in our God? How can you discuss this with a Muslim friend?

_____

_____

_____

_____

_____

4. What are the most cherished names of God that you use in your own personal worship and prayers?

_____

_____

_____

_____

_____

5. How present is the truth of the fatherhood of God in your everyday life? Do you converse with Him as a Father who provides, protects, disciplines and loves you?

_____

_____

_____

_____

_____

Rest on the Road

Talk to God and reflect on how your image of fatherhood is distorted and where it needs to be restored. Come humbly to Him, willing to be counseled, healed, and loved.

_____

_____

_____

_____

_____

_____

_____

_____

_____

_____

Points of Interest

Bible Passages

- I John 3:1-3
- Luke 15:11-32

Books

- Keller, Tim. *The Prodigal God*. Dutton Adult (2008)
- Schneider, Richard H. and Sheikh, Bilquis. *I Dared to Call Him Father: The Miraculous Story of a Muslim Woman's Encounter with God*. Chosen (2003)
- McClung, Floyd. *The Father Heart of God: Experiencing the Depths of His Love for You*. Harvest House Publishers (2004)
- Furguson, Sinclair B. *Children of the Living God*. The Banner of Truth Trust (1989)

Web Sites

- Answering Islam. Who is God? www.answering-islam.org/God/index.html (accessed April 2014)
- Answering Islam. How Muhammad prayed. http://www.answering-islam.org/Shamoun/qiblah.htm (accessed April 2014)

Lesson 7

Jesus the Messiah

Is He the Same as "Isa"?

Islam: Jesus in the Qur'an

Part I: Who is Isa?

The story of Isa according to the Qur'an is found in:

- Sura 3:33-60
- Sura 19:16-36
- Sura 5:110
- Sura 4:157-171

Arab Christians call Jesus **Yasú**

يَسُوع

Muslims call Jesus **Isa**

عِيسَى

You may be surprised to know that Muslims believe in Jesus. They know Him as Isa or Issa. He is mentioned by name in ninety-three places in the Qur'an. He is also addressed with revered titles such as Ibn Maryam (the son of Mary), and the prophet Isa alayhee-al-salaam (Isa peace be on him).

Islam regards itself as the original religion and not a subsequent faith to Judaism and Christianity. The Qur'an and the Hadith teach that all the prophets of the past, such as Abraham, Noah, and David, received the one religion of Islam from Allah (Sura 42:13 and Sura 6:85–87). And Isa, in their view, is no different.

There are two literary sources for "Isa the Prophet." The Qur'an gives a history of his life, while the Hadith collections establish his place in the Muslim understanding of the future. Some of the Muslim beliefs about Jesus are true, while others contradict biblical Christian teachings. We will discuss the main beliefs about Isa, and then compare this supposedly Muslim prophet to Jesus in the Bible in order to highlight the differences and the similarities between the two. Let's begin by telling the story of Isa.

The story of Isa according to the Qur'an and the Hadith

Isa's mother Maryam was the daughter of "Imran" (Amram according to Exodus 6:20) and the sister of Aaron (and Moses—who is never mentioned in connection to Mary's life in the Bible). Maryam was an orphan fostered by Zachariah (father of Yahya, also called John the Baptist). While she was still a virgin, an angel appeared to her and told her that she would bear a son by the power of Allah and that he would be called the Messiah, Isa, son of Maryam. Due to the fact that she was unmarried, she was obligated to conceal her pregnancy. Maryam went eastward into the desert and there, alone in a desolate place, under a palm tree, she gave birth to Isa. While giving birth, she almost died from hunger and thirst, but a voice from within her (the baby) spoke to her and told her to eat dates from the tree. After the birth, Maryam brought the baby Isa to her town. There, the infant inexplicably spoke to the people and told them who he truly was in order to protect his mother from false accusations.

During his life, Isa performed various miracles, including breathing life into clay birds, healing the blind and the lepers, and raising the dead. He also foretold the coming of Muhammad (Sura 61:6). Upon his death, Isa was taken to heaven by Allah; in contrast to Jesus Christ, he was never crucified.

According to the Hadith, "Isa will have an important role in the end times, establishing Islam and making war until he destroys all religions except Islam. He shall kill the Evil One, Dajjal, an apocalyptic anti-Christ figure."[1] In one Hadith attributed to Muhammad we read that no further prophets will come to earth until:

> "Isa returns as a man of medium height, with reddish complexion, wearing two light garments, looking as if drops were falling down from his head although it will not be wet. He will fight for the cause of Islam. He will break the cross, kill pigs, and abolish the poll-tax. Allah will destroy all religions except Islam. He (Isa) will destroy the Evil One and will live on the earth for forty years and then he will die." (Hadith Sunan Abu Dawud, 37:4310; Hadith Sahih Muslim 287)

Where did this story come from?

"Many Qur'anic stories can be traced to Jewish and Christian folktales and other apocryphal literature. For example, a story of Abraham destroying idols (Hadith As-Saffat 37) is found in the Jewish folktale, *The Midrash Rabbah*. The Qur'anic version of the story of Zachariah, father of John the Baptist, is based upon a second-century Christian fable. The story of Jesus being born under a palm tree is also based on a late fable, as is the story of Jesus making clay birds come alive. Everything the Qur'an says about the life of Jesus which is not found in the Bible can be traced to fables."[2]

Assessing the Muslim Isa

- The Qur'an's Isa is not a historical figure. His identity and role as a prophet are based solely on alleged revelations to Muhammad over 600 years after the Jesus of history lived and died.

- Jesus' mother tongue was Aramaic. In His own lifetime Jesus was called *Yeshua* in Aramaic and *Iesous* in Greek. This is the equivalent of calling the same person John when speaking English and Jean when speaking French: *Yeshua* is itself a form of the Hebrew *Yehoshua*, which means "the LORD saves." The Hebrew verb *yasha* means "to save" and "Ya" is the short form of God's personal name "Yahweh." Yeshua of Nazareth was never called *Isa*, the name the Qur'an gives to Him. It is worth noting that Arabic-speaking Christians refer to Jesus as *Yasou* (from *Yeshua*), and never as *Isa*.

- The story of Isa is full of errors. One important historical error is that Maryam the mother of Isa is called the sister of Aaron and also the daughter of Aaron's father Imran (Hebrew Amram). Clearly Muhammad (led by

The name "Isa" does not appear in the Talmud or the Bible. There are several theories on why Muhammad used this for Jesus. Read more at: http://www.answering-islam.org/Responses/Abualrub/true-name-isa.htm

---

[1]Mark Durie, "Isa, the Muslim Jesus" *Answering Islam: A Christian-Muslim Dialog* www.answering-islam.org/authors/durie/islamic_jesus.html (accessed April 2014).
[2]Durie, "Isa, the Muslim Jesus."

Allah) has confused Mary of the New Testament with Miriam of Exodus. The two lived more than a thousand years apart!

Part II: Isa and Jesus, Differences and Similarities

There are five main differences between the true historical Jesus of the Bible and Isa of the Qur'an. Most Muslims are aware of these differences and they reject what the Bible says until the grace of God captures their hearts. There are also ten major similarities that can be used with Muslims as an introduction to who Jesus really is. It is good to start with these similarities, supporting them with Biblical references, to engage Muslims in a discussion about Jesus. Let's do an overview of the five main differences; we will further discuss how Muslims object to these discrepancies about Jesus in another lesson where we focus on apologetics.

Isa of the Qur'an: Differences from Jesus

The Qur'an uses plural pronouns for Allah (We, Our, Us) in a majestic sense, in Arabic called "the royal plural"; denoting the splendor and grandeur of Allah.

Created from Dust	*"Verily, in the sight of God, the nature of Isa is as the nature of Adam, whom He created out of dust and then said unto him, 'Be'— and he is"* (Sura 3:59).
Only a Servant	*"As for Isa, he was nothing but a human being, a servant of Ours whom We had graced with prophethood, and whom We made an example for the children of Israel"* (Sura 43:59).
Not the Son of God	*"...the Christians call Christ the son of Allah. That is a saying from their mouth; (in this) they but imitate what the unbelievers of old used to say. Allah's curse be on them: how they are deluded away from the Truth"* (Sura 9:30).
Not Crucified	*"That they said (in boast), We killed Christ Isa the son of Mary, the Messenger of Allah, but they killed him not, nor crucified him, but so it was made to appear to them..."* (Sura 4:157).
Coming Again	*"Isa returns as 'a man of medium height... He will fight for the cause of Islam."* (Hadith Sunan Abu Dawud, 37:4310).

So according to the Qur'an and the Hadith, Jesus is merely a prophet, created like all other humans, not crucified, and coming to earth again as a Muslim.

Isa of the Qur'an: Similarities to Jesus

The Messiah	"*And their saying: Surely we have killed the Messiah, Isa son of Maryam...*" (Sura 4:157).
Sent by God	"*... And We sent after them in their footsteps Isa, son of Maryam...*" (Sura 5:46).
Born of a Virgin	"*... My Lord! when shall there be a son (born) to me, and man has not touched me?...*" (Sura 3:47).
A Word of God	"*Isa son of Maryam is only a messenger of Allah and His Word ...*" (Sura 4:171).
A Spirit of God	"*... We breathed unto her of Our spirit, and We made her and her son a sign of all peoples ...*" (Sura 21:91).
The Only Sinless Man	"*Abu Huraira said, 'I heard Allah's Apostle saying, 'There is none born among the off-spring of Adam, but Satan touches it... except Mary and her child...'*" (Sahih Al-Bukhari, Volume 4, Book 55, Number 641).
A Worker of Miracles	"*... O Isa... you healed the blind and the leprous by My permission; and when you brought forth the dead by My permission...*" (Sura 5:110).
A Preacher of the Gospel	"*... Isa, son of Maryam, verifying what was before him of the Taurat and We gave him the Injeel in which was guidance and light...*" (Sura 5:46).
Still Alive	"*Nay! Allah took him up to Himself; and Allah is Mighty, Wise*" (Sura 4:158).
Coming Again	"*And Isa shall be a Sign (for the coming of) the Hour (of Judgment)...*" (Sura 43:61).

Although Muslims claim to know the Jesus of the Bible, and may even believe some of the same principles as Christians concerning who our Savior is (the ten similarities), it is clear that what is asserted about Jesus Christ in the Qur'an and the Hadith contradicts the main and most important characteristics of Jesus; He is the Son of God who is with God before the beginning, He is the Savior who died on the cross to redeem sinners and He is the Messiah who is coming again (not as a Muslim). When the Biblical facts are used as the final determining factor, Muslims reject Jesus the One True God, the eternal and unchanging One.

Answers from the Word of God

Side Trip: Jesus of the Bible

Check out these references to see some of what the Bible says about who Jesus is. How does reading these verses make your relationship with Christ more meaningful?

Who Jesus Is	Biblical References	Comments
The Messiah	Matthew 1:1	
Born of a Virgin	Matthew 1:23	
The Word of God	John 1:1, 14	
The Only Sinless Man	I Peter 2:21-22	
Coming Again	Acts 1:9-11	

Main Trip: Where Did Jesus Say, "I Am God?"

Bible Study Passage
John 8:51-58

"'Truly, truly, I say to you, if anyone keeps My word he will never see death.' The Jews said to Him, 'Now we know that You have a demon Abraham died, and the prophets also; and You say, 'If anyone keeps My word, he will never taste of death.' Surely You are not greater than our father Abraham, who died? The prophets died too; whom do You make Yourself out to be?' Jesus answered, 'If I glorify Myself, My glory is nothing; it is My Father who glorifies Me, of whom you say, 'He is our God'; and you have not come to know Him, but I know Him; and if I say that I do not know Him, I will be a liar like you, but I do know Him and keep His word. Your father Abraham rejoiced to see My day, and he saw it and was glad.' So the Jews said to Him, 'You are not yet fifty years old, and have You seen Abraham?' Jesus said to them, 'Truly, truly, I say to you, before Abraham was born, I am.'"

In his famous book *Mere Christianity*, C.S. Lewis says, "A man who was merely a man and said the sort of things Jesus said would not be a great moral teacher.

DARE *TO* EXPLORE

He would either be a lunatic—on the level with a man who says he is a poached egg—or he would be the devil of hell. You must take your choice. Either this was, and is, the Son of God, or else a madman or something worse. You can shut him up for a fool or you can fall at his feet and call him Lord and God. But let us not come with any patronizing nonsense about his being a great human teacher. He has not left that open to us."[3]

Did Jesus ever say in the Bible "I am God?" Muslims often ask this question. Let's search the Bible to find out what Jesus said about Himself and what God the Father reveals about Jesus in His Word.

Jesus' relationship with God the Father

Jesus repeatedly talked about His relationship with God the Father in the four Gospels. He clearly identified Himself as being one with the Father. Here are two main truths Jesus has revealed to us.

- **He who has seen Jesus has seen the Father.** In John 14:9-10, Philip, one of Jesus' disciples, had asked Jesus to show him the Father for confirmation of His divinity. Read what Jesus said to Philip:

  > "Have I been so long with you, and yet you have not come to know Me, Philip? He who has seen Me has seen the Father; how can you say, 'Show us the Father?' Do you not believe that I am in the Father, and the Father is in Me? The words that I say to you I do not speak on My own initiative, but the Father abiding in Me does His works."

- **Jesus and the Father are one.** In John chapter 10, the Jews came to Jesus and asked Him "How long will You keep us in suspense? If you are the Christ, tell us plainly" (John 10:24). Jesus' response was "I told you, and you do not believe; the works that I do in My Father's name, these testify of Me... I and the Father are one" (John 10:25, 30). Later in that same exchange Jesus confirmed to them "the Father is in me, and I in the Father" (John 10:38).

What did Jesus reveal about Himself?

- **He is the only way to the Father.** At the last supper Christ was telling His disciples about His coming death. When Thomas, looking for comfort and direction, said to Jesus "'Lord, we do not know where You are going, how do we know the way?' Jesus said to him: 'I am the way, the truth, and the life. No one comes to the Father but by me'" (John 14:5–6).

- **He is the Son of God.** In Mark chapter 14 when Christ was on trial before the high priests, they questioned Him, "'Are You the Christ, the Son of the Blessed One?' And Jesus said, 'I am; and you shall see the Son of Man sitting

---

[3]C.S. Lewis, *Mere Christianity,* (New York: Macmillan, 1960) 56.

at the right hand of power, and coming with the clouds of heaven.'" Also, in Luke chapter 22 they asked Him, "'Are You the Son of God, then?' And He said to them, 'Yes, I am.'"

What Did God the Father Reveal About Jesus?

Just as Jesus identified Himself as one with the Father, God the Father identified Jesus as His own. The Father repeats and reinforces the claims Christ has made about Himself; here are two examples.

- **Jesus is the Son.** In Matthew 3:16-17, Jesus came to John the Baptist to be baptized. "As soon as Jesus was baptized, he went up out of the water. At that moment heaven was opened, and he saw the Spirit of God descending like a dove and lighting on him. And a voice from heaven said, 'This is my Son, whom I love; with him I am well pleased.'" Also, in Mark 9:7, the transfiguration story, God announced clearly: "This is my Son, whom I love. Listen to him!"

- **Jesus is Mighty God.** God inspired Isaiah to prophesy that the promised Messiah would not be a mere human being but rather would be God himself. We read in Isaiah 9:6 "For to us a child is born, to us a son is given, and the government will be on his shoulders. And he will be called Wonderful Counselor, Mighty God, Everlasting Father, Prince of Peace."

Jesus is God

Throughout His ministry, Jesus proves that He is God by doing what the True God can do.

- **Jesus controls nature.** He stilled a raging storm of wind and waves on the Sea of Galilee. He turned water into wine, fed 5,000 people from five loaves and two fish, gave a grieving widow back her only son by raising him from the dead, and brought to life the dead daughter of a shattered father. To an old friend He said, "Lazarus, come forth!" and dramatically raised him from the dead (John 11:43).

- **Jesus demonstrates the Creator's power over sickness and disease.** He caused the lame to walk, the dumb to speak, and the blind to see.

- **Jesus forgives sin.** Only God can forgive sin and yet we read that Jesus forgave sins. Therefore, Jesus is God. In the story of the paralyzed man, in Luke chapter 5, when Jesus saw the faith of his friends, He said to the man,

    "'Friend, your sins are forgiven you.' The scribes and the Pharisees began to reason, saying, 'Who is this man who speaks blasphemies? Who can forgive sins, but God alone?' But Jesus, aware of their reasonings, answered and said to them, 'Why are you reasoning in your hearts?' Which is easier, to say, 'Your sins have been forgiven you,' or

to say, 'Get up and walk?' But, so that you may know that the Son of Man has authority on earth to forgive sins, He said to the paralytic 'I say to you, get up, and pick up your stretcher and go home.' Immediately he got up before them, and picked up what he had been lying on, and went home glorifying God. They were all struck with astonishment and began glorifying God; and they were filled with fear, saying, 'We have seen remarkable things today'" (Luke 5:20-26).

- **Jesus rose from the dead.** The most important biblical authentication of Jesus' claim to deity was His resurrection from the dead. Jesus predicted five times that He would die, and that three days later He would rise from the dead and appear to the disciples. "From that time Jesus began to show His disciples that He must go to Jerusalem, and suffer many things from the elders and chief priests and scribes, and be killed, and be raised up on the third day" (Matthew 16:21).

- **Jesus grants eternal life.** Jesus shows that He is God by granting eternal life; the life which God himself has, to all who believe in Him. Jesus said: "Truly, truly, I say to you, an hour is coming and now is, when the dead will hear the voice of the Son of God, and those who hear will live. For just as the Father has life in Himself, even so He gave to the Son also to have life in Himself" (John 5:25-26).

- **Jesus receives worship as God.** The Bible insists in more than five hundred passages that worship should be given to God alone. Yet, Jesus receives worship in several places in the Bible. The Persian Magi seek to worship Him (Matthew 2:2, 11). The disciples worship Him (Matthew 14:33, 28:9, 17; Luke 24:52; John 20:28). God tells the angels to worship the Son (Hebrews 1:6). Heavenly beings and those gathered in heaven worship "the Lamb who was slain" (Revelation 5:12-14).

This is the mighty God whom we worship; the Risen Savior, The Son of God, Jesus Christ, who is one with the Father.

Probing Deeper

1. When did you first hear about Jesus? What do you remember?

_____

_____

_____

_____

_____

2. Share your reflections on the story of the birth of Isa according to the Qur'an and the Hadith.

_____

_____

_____

_____

_____

3. Which claims about Isa surprised you the most?

_____

_____

_____

_____

4. From what you have read in this lesson, how does Jesus differ from any other prophet or teacher?

_____

_____

_____

_____

5. In your own words explain the importance of the resurrection of Jesus within the plan of salvation.

_____

_____

_____

_____

_____

Rest on the Road

Talk to God about your personal relationship with Jesus and the difference He has made in your life.   Meditate on what He did for you on the Cross and then pray for the Muslims who do not know Christ as the Son of God and the Savior.

_____

_____

_____

_____

_____

_____

_____

_____

_____

_____

_____

Points of Interest

Bible Passages

- Isaiah 53
- John 1
- Luke 22, 23, 24

Books

- Lewis, C.S. *Mere Christianity.* Macmillan (1960)

Web Sites

- Answering Islam: A Christian-Muslim Dialog. Who is Jesus. http://www. answering-islam.org/Who/index.html (accessed April 2014)

Lesson Notes

The story of Isa according to the Qur'an is found in:

- Sura 3:33-60
- Sura 19:16-36
- Sura 5:110
- Sura 4:157-171

Lesson 8

Women

In Islam and In God's Eyes

Islam: Muhammad and Women

Muslims all over the globe have contradictory convictions about women. Those who are exposed to western civilizations are more "liberal" in their views towards women. These Muslims adopt the West's beliefs and claim that these come from the true origin of Islam, Muhammad and his teaching. They choose Qur'anic verses and Hadith sections that please them, but ignore the ones that specifically contradict the principle that women are equal to men. On the other hand, fundamental, or "conservative" Muslims, the majority of whom resist the western view of women (even though they might be physically living in a western country), proudly practice the degrading way Muhammad has taught the followers of Islam to treat women. To understand the true plight of the women in Islam we have to first look at the family life of the founder, whom the followers of Islam cling to and imitate in their everyday practices.

Part I: Muhammad's wives

We mentioned in another lesson that Muhammad had approximately sixteen wives during his lifetime, in addition to the maidens who were captured as the spoils of war. These female slaves were not considered wives because Muhammad neither gave them a dowry, nor established a contract of marriage with them.

Muslims boast that their prophet stayed true to his first wife Khadijah until she died. They forget that during that period, Muhammad was a poor, twenty-five-year-old, married to his employer, who happened to be extremely wealthy. After her death, Muhammad revealed his true nature, but only Muslim scholars are familiar with this fact. The majority of Muslims know only as much as their leaders tell them about their prophet, who is portrayed to them as an innocent, pure, godly man, wearing a white robe, and spending most of his time in prayers, and in helping the weak and the poor. This is the image that most Muslims fall in love with and sing praises to, but this picture quickly dissolves as soon as they themselves start reading and searching for the truth, and find the deception behind Muhammad's public image.

Let's look at some of Muhammad's wives and how he obtained them.

Aisha—the child wife and most beloved

Muhammad married the little girl Aisha, the daughter of his friend Abu Bakr, when he was fifty-three years old. Aisha herself narrated in the Hadith:

> "The Messenger of [Allah] married me in the tenth year after his prophet-hood, three years before the Migration as I was six years old. I was nine years old when he consummated the marriage with me. The Messenger of [Allah] married me when I was still playing with the girls. I did not know that the Messenger of [Allah] married me until my mother took me and locked me up in the house. Then I realized that I was married" (Hadith Tabaqat, 8:58, Hadith Abu Dawud No. 34).

Zainab—Wife by special revelation

Muhammad fell in love with his daughter-in-law Zainab, wife of his adopted Son (Zaid Ibn Haritha). One day Muhammad went to Zaid's house on some business, but his son was not home. Muhammad cast his eyes accidentally on Zainab, who was then in a dress which discovered her beauty to advantage, and was so smitten at the sight, that he could not stop crying out, "[Allah] be praised, who turneth the hearts of men as he pleaseth!"[1] Zainab was flattered by the remark of Muhammad and conveyed the comment to her husband Zaid. After reflecting on this, and fearing his father Muhammad, Zaid determined to divorce her so that Muhammad could marry her. After a short period, Muhammad claimed that he received an order from Allah to marry Zainab. This revelation seemed designed to give Allah's approval so that no scandal would arise out of the situation. Hence the Qur'an states regarding this episode; *"There is no fault in the Prophet, touching what [Allah] has ordained for him"* (Sura 33:38).

After this incident, Mohammad abolished the "heresy of adoption", claiming it was a detestable pre-Islamic practice: *"... nor has He made your adopted sons your sons. Such is only your (manner of) speech by your mouths. But Allah tells you the Truth, and He shows the (right) Way"* (Sura 33:4).

It is worth noting that apart from Aisha and Zainab, all of Muhammad's wives were either women of ally tribes or widows whose husbands and families were killed during Muhammad's wars. These women were held captive and brought to Muhammad as part of the spoils of his newly conquered territories. One of these captive women was Safiyya the Jew.

---

[1] *The History of Al-Tabari: The Victory of Islam*, translated by Michael Fishbein (State University of New York Press, Albany, 1997), Volume VIII, pp. 2-3.

Safiyya Bint Huyay, the captive Jew

Muhammad waged war against the Jewish tribe Khaibar. He summarily conquered this people and collected the profits of war, including many human captives. One of his warriors, Dihya, came to Muhammad and said: "O Allah's Prophet! Give me a slave girl from the captives." The Prophet said, "Go and take any slave girl." He took Safiya bint Huyay. A man named Anas came to the Prophet and said, "O Allah's Apostle! You gave Safiya bint Huyay to Dihya and she is the chief mistress of the tribes of Quraiza and An-Nadir and she befits none but you." So the Prophet said, "Bring him along with her." So Dihya came with her and when the Prophet saw her, he said to Dihya, "Take any slave girl other than her from the captives." Anas then told that Muhammad *manumitted* [set free from slavery] her and married her. Anas was asked by some Muslims, "What did the Prophet pay her as *Mahr* dowry?" He said, "Her self was her Mahr for he manumitted her and then married her." (Excerpts from Hadith Sahih Bukhari, Book 8, No. 367) In other words, Safiyya's freedom from slavery and her marriage to Muhammad served as her dowry.

Part II: Women According to Muhammad and the Qur'an

Muslims claim that Islam and Muhammad elevated the position of women in the world. They highlight the few positive changes that concern women, which Muhammad brought to the tribes in the Arabian Peninsula, but they try to forget the major teachings of Muhammad that still degrade Muslim women to this day. In order to be fair in presenting an entire overview of the teachings of Islam regarding its treatment of women, here are the positive changes that took place during Muhammad's time:

Islam's Positive Attitudes Toward Women

Muhammad abolished the horrible practice of female *Wa'ad* (burying female infants alive) which was prevalent among the pagan Arabs. This was Muhammad's only substantial positive act towards women.

Muhammad confirmed some good principles which other peoples already practiced towards women, especially Christians and Jews, and he ordered Muslims to follow them. These practices include:
• Respect towards the mother as second to worship
• Protection of the daughters' and sisters' honor from illicit relationships
• Financial provision for the women in one's family.

Islam's Negative Attitudes Toward Women

It is sad to say that the oppressive teachings concerning women that Muhammad introduced not only outweigh the good ones, but they also have caused and continue to bring catastrophic consequences to the lives of the Muslim women. Without overwhelming you with countless agonizing details, here is a list of the major negative principles of Islam toward women. We will quote the Qur'an as well as Muhammad from the Hadith.

1. In marriage, the Muslim woman:

  a. Is bought by a dowry to become a wife. (Hadith Abu Dawud 848, 849)

  b. Can be beaten by her husband for any reason. *"Righteous women are therefore obedient… And those you fear may be rebellious admonish; banish them to their couches, and beat them…"* (Sura 4:34).

  c. Can be divorced by one phrase from her husband "You are divorced."[2]

  d. Can expect up to three additional women to share her husband. *"Marry woman of your choice in twos' threes' or fours' but if ye fear that ye shall not be able to deal justly, (with them), then only one"* (Sura 4:3).

  e. Cannot keep her children when divorced if they are older than seven years or if she remarries.[3]

2. In other areas, the Muslim woman:

  a. Is half in witness. *"Two men should witness, but if not two men, then one man, and two women so that if one of the two women should err, the other will remind her"* (Sura 2:282).

  b. Is half in inheritance. *"God instructs you concerning your children; for a male the like of the portion of two females, and if there be women above two, then let them have two-thirds of what (the deceased) leaves… "* (Sura 4:12).

  c. Her body is Awra. It brings shame and degradation. "Ali reported the Prophet saying: 'Women have ten (awrat). When she gets married, the husband covers one, and when she dies the grave covers the ten'" (Kanz-el-'Ummal, Vol. 22, Hadith No. 858).

  d. Lacks in intelligence. "Muhammad said: 'Isn't the witness of a woman equal to half of that of a man?' The women said: 'Yes.' He said: 'This is because of the deficiency of her mind'" (Hadith Sahih Al-Bukhari Number 2658).

  e. Is deficient in gratitude "I was shown the Hell-fire and that the majority of its dwellers were women who were ungrateful." (Sahih Bukhari vol. 1 Hadith No. 28).

> **Women negating Men's prayers**
>
> Women can negate a man's prayer by walking in front of him. Therefore, women are required to pray in the back of the mosque or at home. Sahih Al-Bukhari Hadith - 1.490

[2]Islam QA, *Divorce*, http://www.islam-qa.com/en/cat/358 (accessed April 2014).

[3]Overview Of Shari'a and Prevalent Customs In Islamic Societies - Divorce and Child Custody http://www.expertlaw.com/library/family_law/islamic_custody-3.html#80 (accessed April 2014).

f. Is inferior to man. *"Men are the maintainers of women because Allah has made some of them to excel others and because they spend out of their property..."* (Sura 4:34).

3. **In religion, the Muslim woman:**
   a. Lacks in understanding religion. (Hadith Bukhari Volume 1, No. 301)
   b. Is evil and spoils men's prayers. (Hadith Bukhari Volume 1, No. 490)
   c. Is expected to pray at her house. (Fiqh-us-Sunnah Volume 2 No. 50)
   d. Is most likely heading to hell. "The Prophet said, '... I looked at Hell and saw that the majority of its inhabitants were women'" (Hadith Bukhari Volume 4, Book 54, No. 464).
   e. If she goes to paradise, here is what she is promised: "Muhammad said: 'In Paradise there is a pavilion made of a single hollow pearl sixty miles wide, in each corner of which there are wives who will not see those in the other corners; and the believers (men) will visit and enjoy them'" (Hadith Sahih Al-Bukhari Number 4879).

Muslim women live by these practices not only in Muslim countries but also in the West among their families and in their communities. The majority of them do not have a voice or an opportunity to oppose the men in their families, or to find help from their religious leaders, leaving them with no safe means of escape. However, through the media and personal contact, God is bringing hope to many of these Muslim women. Thousands of them secretly accept Jesus but continue to live as Muslims.

Answers from the Word of God

Side Trip: Marriage According to the Bible

We have read how Islam views marriage and how Muslim husbands treat their wives. Let's look at God's plan for marriage in the Bible. Look up these verses and summarize some of the biblical principles of marriage.

Verses	Summary of the Principle
Genesis 2:24, Matthew 19:5-6	
Genesis 2:18	
Ephesians 5:25	
Malachi 2:13-16, Mark 10:11-12	
Matthew 22:30	

Main Trip: Mary Magdalene the Disciple

Bible Study Passage
Luke 8:1-3

> "Soon afterwards, He began going around from one city and village to another, proclaiming and preaching the kingdom of God. The twelve were with Him, and also some women who had been healed of evil spirits and sicknesses: Mary who was called Magdalene, from whom seven demons had gone out, and Joanna the wife of Chuza, Herod's steward, and Susanna, and many others who were contributing to their support out of their private means."

Christ and His Women Followers
Mary Magdalene is mentioned twelve times in the Bible. Her life is a good example of how Jesus regarded women over 2000 years ago. Mary Magdalene became a disciple of Christ after He had driven seven demons out of her. She and the other disciples followed Jesus throughout His ministry, and she was one of the witnesses at His resurrection.

Mary Magdalene in the New Testament

As a disciple of Jesus
Luke 8:1-3

At the crucifixion
Mark 15:40-41, Luke 23:49, Matthew 27:55-56, John 19:25

Prepares the body of Jesus for burial
Luke 23:55-56, Matthew 27:61

A witness to the Resurrection
Mark 16:1-11, Luke 24:1-11, Matthew 28:1-10

Meets Jesus at the empty tomb
John 20:1-18

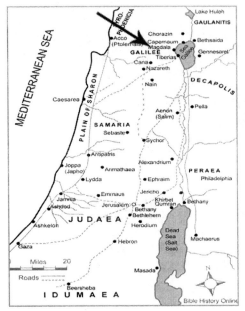

Mary Magdalene was from Magdala, a village on the northwest side of the Sea of Galilee. Magdala was a thriving town, focused on fishing and the production of smoked fish in large quantities. It was also known as a manufacturing center for fine wool and woolen dyes. There is no account of where or when Mary Magdalene was set free from the demons but we do know it was in the first period of Jesus' ministry. Magdala was geographically quite close to Nazareth and Cana, and Jesus probably visited the region a number of times. At some point in her life, Mary met Jesus and He healed her. The fact that she was healed is referenced several times in the Bible, such as in Luke 8:1-3.

Although she is believed by some to have been an immoral woman, there is no biblical evidence of that. What we do know from the Bible is that Mary Magdalene was a single woman of financial means, widowed, divorced, or never married. She devoted her life and resources to serving Jesus and His disciples. She may have even been the informal leader of Christ's female followers but there is no clear indication of that.

Mary Magdalene is a wonderful model of a godly woman who lived a life of creative and productive service. She focused her efforts solely on Jesus Christ and served Him faithfully during His life, at His death, and after His resurrection.

From this information about Mary Magdalene we get a picture of how Jesus included women in His ministry and did not differentiate between men and women in any way.

Equal in Creation

Jesus cared enough for Mary Magdalene to take the time to drive the demons out of her so she could become a healthy woman. In this way Jesus shows that women are equal to men in nature and spirit. The Bible affirms that women are equal in value, have the same essence, and share the same divine image that men do. They also share with men sovereignty over the physical creation:

> "Then God said, 'Let Us make man in Our image, according to Our likeness; and let them rule over the fish of the sea and over the birds of the sky and over the cattle and over all the earth, and over every creeping thing that creeps on the earth.' God created man in His own image, in the image of God He created him; male and female He created them" (Genesis 1:26-27).

Jesus demonstrated for us that He values equally the lives of women and men when He took the time to stop and heal them of their ailments, to make them whole.

Equal in Salvation

Jesus did not only heal Mary Magdalene physically and emotionally from the seven demons that possessed her, but He also healed her spiritually. She became a woman not ruled by sin, but by a desire to serve God with her whole heart. This is God's desire for all men and women. While we will not be truly free from sin until we reach Heaven, we can live out our lives here on earth without being ruled by our flawed human nature. Women are equal to men in salvation; God loves women and redeems them along with men. Christ died for both men and women, making all of them co-heirs of the kingdom:

> "For you are all sons of God through faith in Christ Jesus. For all of you who were baptized into Christ have clothed yourselves with Christ. There is neither Jew nor Greek, there is neither slave nor free man, there is neither male nor female; for you are all one in Christ Jesus. And if you belong to Christ, then you are Abraham's descendants, heirs according to promise" (Galatians 3:26-29).

Jesus cared for women's spiritual health as well as their physical health and took the time to bring life to their souls. The Samaritan woman is a wonderful example of how much Jesus cared for women's salvation. See John 4:7–38.

Equal in Ministry

Jesus did not prevent Mary Magdalene or the other women from following Him, serving with Him, and tending to His needs, and neither did any of the disciples. There is no indication that the female participants of Jesus' group were viewed as unusual, or looked down upon. This shows that Jesus knows that women are not lacking in intelligence or in spiritual understanding. They have the ability to manage their own affairs in all areas, including those of finances, ministry, and society. This does not mean that Jesus calls women to a radical feminist movement, but He confirms the equal value of women and men in God's eyes. Although women's roles might be different from those of men, this definitely does not mean they are of less value.

There are several examples of women in ministry in the New Testament. For example, Priscilla and her husband Aquilla were both tentmakers and missionaries to the Jews (Acts 18). In Acts 9:32-43, Dorcas ministered to other women and "was abounding with deeds of kindness and charity which she continually did" (Acts 9:36). Paul appreciated Phoebe's ministry and mentioned her several times in his letters; she was a servant of the church at Cenchrea (Romans 16:1). These first-century Christian women worked faithfully and diligently at proclaiming the Gospel to the least and the lost and in serving the body of believers.

Equal in Responsibility

Mary Magdalene was a part of the most important story in history. Not only did she witness Jesus' crucifixion, but she also saw the empty tomb, and had a one-on-one encounter with the resurrected Lord. She was one of the first to realize that the Resurrection had occurred and Jesus gave her a particular message to take to the other disciples: "… go to My brethren and say to them, 'I ascend to My Father and your Father, and My God and your God'" (John 20:17). Women serving as primary witnesses and messengers do not seem unusual to us today, but it was a revolutionary concept in the first century. The testimony of women was not given the same weight as men's, either personally or in a law court. When the Bible described Mary Magdalene and the other women as the first witnesses of the Resurrection, it makes an important statement about the status of women within Christianity. Mary Magdalene in particular is entrusted with a most important message for the disciples, the message of Jesus' Resurrection. Jesus believed that Mary Magdalene heard correctly, that she could tell the message precisely, and that she would be believed by the disciples. She had credibility, even as a woman in that time.

In Luke 24:33-49 we learn that the disciples and those that were with them (this included the women followers) were visited by Jesus after His Resurrection. In Acts 1:8 Jesus gave this same gathered group these instructions: "but you will receive power when the Holy Spirit has come upon you; and you shall be My witnesses both in Jerusalem, and in all Judea and Samaria, and even to the remotest part of the earth." All of Christ's followers, both men and women, those who witnessed His earthly ministry and those who follow Him now, two thousand years later, have the responsibility of sharing the Gospel.

Jesus does not discriminate between men and women. They are equal in creation, salvation, ministry, and responsibility. Men and women may have different gifts and different ways to express them, but we are all part of the great story of Salvation. Women were created in God's image and are equal partakers in the redemption story. As a result, women have an important place in ministry and in evangelism. And just as Mary Magdalene proclaimed the good news of the Resurrection to the disciples, we, both men and women, must proclaim that same message to the lost world.

Probing Deeper

1. Who are some of the godly women that helped shape your view of women?

_____

_____

_____

_____

2. Express what went through your mind as you read about how Muhammad
   treated women in his own life.

_____

_____

_____

_____

_____

3. Share how you've seen some of these Muslim attitudes about women played
   out in your own culture, community, or family life. Are you aware that
   Satan is the source of these negative attitudes?

_____

_____

_____

_____

_____

4. Before you read this lesson, what did you know about Mary Magdalene's
   life? Did you learn anything new?

_____

_____

_____

_____

5. As a woman, are you aware of your spiritual responsibilities and are you able to use your spiritual gifts in your church and community? As a man, are you encouraging the women in your life to serve and minister as Jesus did?

_____

_____

_____

_____

_____

Rest on the Road

Do you have a distorted view of women from your past that you need to pray about? Use this space to talk to God about how you feel and allow the Holy Spirit to minister to you, correcting, encouraging, and healing.

_____

_____

_____

_____

_____

_____

_____

_____

_____

_____

_____

Points of Interest

Bible Passages

- Ephesians 5:22-33

- I Samuel 25:2-44: Abigail the wise woman

Books

- Ankerberg, John and Caner, Emir. *The Truth About Islam & Women.* Harvest House Publishers (2009)

Lesson 9

Loving Muslims

Building Social Bridges

Building Social Bridges with Muslims

Part I: Understanding Ministry to Muslims

Most of us believe that it is impossible for a Muslim to renounce Islam and choose Christ. Not only do Muslims tell us this, but so does the majority of mainstream media (the exception being media produced by ministries who are involved in reaching Muslims). The truth is that in the past twenty-five years, more Muslims have come to know the Lord than in the entire fourteen previous centuries of Islam. Due to the high level of availability of internet, satellite TV, and short wave radio, contemporary Muslims are more exposed to other religions than Muslims of the past. In spite of this, Muslims are still one of the most unreached and under reached groups in the world. Over 80% of the 1.5 billion Muslims have not yet heard the Good News of the Gospel.

The obvious reason for this is that reaching Muslims can be a lengthy and intensive process. A missionary to Muslims needs to:

- Learn apologetics relevant to Muslims
- Study the Arabic language and the religion of Islam
- Understand how Muslim culture and social norms differ from our own
- Minister in secret
- Be willing as a missionary to Muslims to face dangerous persecution, severe spiritual warfare, and sometimes death

We often forget that in Muslim countries:

- Christian evangelism is prohibited
- Christian churches and pastors are watched and persecuted
- Tent-making ministries are challenging to establish and maintain
- Most Muslims are afraid of interacting publicly with Christians

The good news is that God is bringing Muslims to our backyard from all over the Muslim world: Saudi Arabia, Indonesia, Iran, Syria, Malaysia, China, etc. And these Muslims are reachable for these two main reasons:

- They have the freedom to think for themselves and ask questions without being accused of infidelity.

Muslims are not so much resistant as neglected

Only 3% of the church's entire missionary force is currently ministering to Muslims. There is one Christian missionary for every half-million Muslims

- They experience less influence from the Muslim community, and more opportunities to meet true followers of Christ who can provide them with the Word of God and invite them to church.

This is why we have been studying about Islam in the previous lessons. Now we have arrived at the core of our goal, which is to reach Muslims whom we meet in our everyday lives; at work, in the neighborhood, at special events, in the store, at the gym, and in the classroom.

The Gap

In the past lessons, you have been studying what Muslims believe, how they pray, and how they look at life in general. However, even with a grasp of what the Muslim religion entails, you might still feel uncomfortable in approaching a Muslim.

One of the main reasons Christians hesitate to take the first step in evangelizing to a Muslim is the gap that exists between the Western and the Muslim cultures. Often times, Christians feel that they personally do not know any Muslims well enough to predict their reactions, or to avoid offending them and making them angry. Do not be discouraged, the remedy for this problem is already underway: the more we understand the Muslims' culture and values, the more this seemingly endless gap will shrink.

To start, here are the main cultural/values gaps that we must understand and address. While you are reading this comparison, try to determine which of these values apply to you. Many of these Western Values are not in agreement with the Word of God but we often adhere to them simply because we are Westerners. You might also notice that as Christians, we share some values with the Muslims. These values, such as hospitality, are Bible based but some of us have wandered away from them. As you read the list try to discern those that you cling to which are not biblical and pray for God's help to overcome them.

If you feel the need to study Muslim culture and values in more detail, we have suggested additional resources in the "Points of Interest" section at the end of this lesson.

Muslim Values	Western Values
Honor: A Muslim's good acts bring honor and pride to the family and the community	**Respect:** A person's good acts gain him a good reputation and respect in his places of influence
Shame: A Muslim's shortcomings bring shame to the entire community, which has the right to punish him in order to wipe out the shame	**Guilt:** A person's mistakes make him guilty, and he is punished by authorities in the sphere of the error, e.g., work, law enforcement, church, school, etc.
Saving face: Maintaining a good appearance in front of others is more important than demanding justice, even if this hurts one's own family	**Demanding Rights:** When there is injustice, demanding one's rights is a priority even if it means the injustice becomes public
Communal: The collective interest is more important than the individual's rights	**Individualistic:** A singular person's well-being is more important than the community's interests
Shared Aims: A Muslim must adopt the goals of the community and make them his own	**Personal Goals:** Personal success is a priority and therefore goals are chosen by the individual
Loyalty to Community System: Loyalty is not to the personal conscience but to what the community decides is lawful	**Loyalty to Personal Beliefs:** Personal beliefs and adopted principles are the base of one's values
Hospitality: Generosity and hospitality are two major characteristics of a community-based culture	**Privacy:** One's own comfort, enjoyment, and convenience are priorities in an individualistic culture
Extended Family Influence: In addition to the nuclear family, the larger family influences a Muslim's life: uncles, aunts, cousins, grandparents, and so on	**Nuclear Family:** The influence of the family has boundaries, and is usually limited to the parents and siblings

Part II: Keys to Building Social Bridges

We want to encourage you to take the first step in building a bridge of friendship and trust between you and your Muslim neighbors. To achieve this goal, you do not have to be a scholar of Islam, or an expert in understanding their culture. God will direct your path and will give you the wisdom and insight required once you prayerfully take the first step. Here are some suggested ways to build social bridges with the Muslim.

1.Take the first step

Sometimes it is not easy for us to take the first step, but you must be aware of the fact that your Muslim neighbor does not know if you welcome his or her friendship. We have to put Muslims at ease, make them feel welcome, accept them as they are, and be sensitive to their traditions. Make it you responsibility to take the first step. For example, you can start by asking:

- Would you like to come over for a cup of coffee or tea after the children go to school?
- We have been working together for quite some time now and I would like to get to know you more. Are you free to have lunch together tomorrow?
- Can your daughter come to my daughter's birthday next week? If you have a special diet, I would be glad to make sure we have something for her.

2. Actively look for an opportunity

Always be on the lookout for the right time to invite the Muslim for a cup of coffee or a casual meal. Birthday parties, holidays, Thanksgiving, and Christmas are good times to show the Muslim how you celebrate and who you socialize with. Make the Muslim feel welcome in your home and show respect to his or her traditions and diet. Most Muslims do not eat pork, or any products that might have lard or pork gelatin (like marshmallows), and most do not drink alcohol. Of course, the more westernized Muslims might have left these traditions behind, so make sure to ask first before offering any food or drink.

3. Show practical care

When you start a relationship with a Muslim family, several opportunities might arise where you can truly prove your authentic love and care for them. They might be new in the area or the country.

- Help their children with homework.
- Help them with English by directing them to a church in your community that offers ESL.

Your friendships with Muslims should always be:

A man with a man

A woman with a woman

Family with family

Avoid inter-gender relationships

To find Islamic businesses and resources in your area use www.islamicfinder.org

- Help them fill out job applications, school papers, or other official documents.
- Be there for them and let them feel and know that they are welcome to visit you at home and that you would like to come visit them and experience their culture.

4. Invite them to church

This step usually comes after the friendship has been established. However, if your Muslim friend initiates and shows interest in your place of worship, do not hesitate to take him or her to your church. Special occasions in the church are very good times to invite your Muslim friends for the first time, such as Christmas, vacation Bible school, women's teas or men's breakfast events. Remember that Muslims do not have praise and worship in their mosques, so to experience a collective outpouring of worship in the sanctuary might be a lifetime experience for them, where for the first time in their lives they feel the presence of God. After church, take the time to help the Muslim reflect on what happened at church, and try to answer questions he or she might have.

5. Pray, pray, pray

In Ephesians 6:12 we read "… our struggle is not against flesh and blood but against the rulers, against the authorities, against the power of this dark world, and against the spiritual forces of evil in the heavenly realms." Remember that your spiritual conflict is not against the Muslim people, but against Satan himself, who will try to thwart your efforts. Therefore, it is important to ask your Christian friends to support you with prayer while you are on this journey.

Follow up and never give up

When you start a relationship with a Muslim, do not stop in the middle of the road. This ministry is not easy, as it takes time and effort, and sometimes entails years of building trust and love. At times you might feel you are not getting anywhere. If you should experience this feeling of futility, wait upon the Lord, pray, renew your strength, pick up the phone, and show your Muslim friend that you care for him or her, that you want to be involved in their lives, and that you love them.

Answers from the Word of God

Side Trip: Live the Story

Think of some practical ways that will help you make connections with each of these types of Muslims you may have contact with now or in the future.

Muslims you may have contact with	First steps to making connection
Family across the street	
Male colleague at work	
Children at school	
A veiled Muslim cashier	
Mosque in your community	

Main Trip: Jesus' Practical Ministry

Bible Study Passage

John 1:35-40

> "Again the next day John was standing with two of his disciples and he looked at Jesus as He walked, and said, 'Behold, the Lamb of God!' The two disciples heard him speak, and they followed Jesus. And Jesus turned and saw them following, and said to them, 'What do you seek?' They said to Him, 'Rabbi (which translated means Teacher), where are you staying?' He said to them, 'Come, and you will see.' So they came and saw where He was staying; and they stayed with Him that day, for it was about the tenth hour. One of the two who heard John speak and followed Him, was Andrew, Simon Peter's brother."

Jesus and hospitality

Jesus' earthly ministry was out in the community, not elevated above the troubled masses in an ivory tower or temple. He lived among ordinary people and got involved in their everyday lives. Jesus gave every moment of His life to loving people and to meeting their needs. One of the precious examples that Jesus models for us is how He hosted some of His first disciples. We read in our Bible passage the question that the two disciples asked Him: "Rabbi,

109

where are you staying?" From this question Jesus was able to understand that these disciples wanted to have a closer relationship with Him, to get to know Him, eat with Him, and to sit and talk with Him. Jesus could have told them where He was staying, chatted with them for a while, and then moved on, but instead, He invited them to come with Him to where he was staying, responding: "Come and you will see." This is one of the rare times that the Holy Spirit records in such detail what happened next: "…and they stayed with Him that day, for it was about the tenth hour." It was 4 p.m. (as we express time), and Jesus spent the rest of the day with the two disciples. According to the traditions of that day, Jesus probably offered them water to wash their feet, food and drink, and made a place for them to sleep. What greater example than this of our Lord do we need of how to build warm relationships with others by opening our homes and our lives? Notice that Jesus invited these men that very day. He made time for them, was available in order to draw them closer to Himself, and to help them trust Him and believe in Him.

Hospitality and personal engagement are contradictory to our Western way of living. How many Westerners would invite strangers back to their homes to stay the night? However, as Christians, hospitality should be a natural part of our lives. The Word of God commands us to show our faith through hospitality.

> "Let love of the brethren continue. Do not neglect to show hospitality to strangers, for by this some have entertained angels without knowing it. Remember the prisoners, as though in prison with them, and those who are ill-treated, since you yourselves also are in the body" (Hebrews 13:1-3).

> "Be devoted to one another in brotherly love; give preference to one another in honor; not lagging behind in diligence, fervent in spirit, serving the Lord; rejoicing in hope, persevering in tribulation, devoted to prayer, contributing to the needs of the saints, practicing hospitality" (Romans 12:10-13).

Jesus in the community

In John chapter 17, Jesus prayed for His disciples and for us that we would be engaged in our community just as He was engaged in the world. "As You sent Me into the world, I also have sent them into the world" (John 17:18).

When Jesus was on earth He not only lived in the community, but actively participated in it as well. He shared the people's joys and sorrows; He attended events and went to the marketplace; He met people where they lived, worked, and gathered. The wedding at Cana (John 2) was the first event in Jesus' public ministry that the Bible records. Weddings were festive community occasions in the Jewish culture. Jesus, as a resident of Galilee, would have been a part of

this wedding celebration just like the rest of the neighborhood. It is significant that our first picture of Jesus' ministry occurred at a community event.

After the wedding at Cana, Jesus traveled to different towns and cities to minister to the people around him. In the next few chapters of the book of John we read about Jesus connecting with ordinary people in the places where they worked and lived, such as:

- In the market place at the temple (John 2:13–25)
- The Pool of Bethesda where Jesus healed the lame man (John 5)
- In Samaria, a hostile environment, where He changed the life of the Samaritan woman (John 4)
- On the road, healing the man born blind (John 9)
- In Bethany, sharing in the sorrows of His friends and raising Lazarus from the dead (John 11)

How should we follow Jesus' example? Building relationships with people and being a blessing to them is the key. For most of us, it is much easier to write a check to a mission organization than to give of our time and of ourselves to meet the needs around us. It is also much more comfortable to spend our time only with people who think like us, but this can lead to unintentional isolation from a world of lost souls in need of Jesus' love, Muslims included. Acting outside our comfort zone is a challenge that Christ calls us to take seriously if we want to be His true disciples, His hands and feet in this world. This is part of our Christian walk, to be salt and light where we live, and this cannot be achieved if we shut ourselves inside our comfortable homes.

Jesus said: "Let your light shine before men in such a way that they may see your good works, and glorify your Father who is in heaven" (Matthew 5:16). Remember, no light can shine as brightly as when it is out in the open, available for all to look upon.

Jesus meets the needs of the community

Jesus' connection with people wasn't limited to those who sought Him. He actively reached out to the sick, the hurting, and the lost.

- When He saw a mother weeping for the loss of her only son, He stopped in the middle of the road to bring hope and life to that family. "When the Lord saw her, He felt compassion for her, and said to her, 'Do not weep.' And He came up and touched the coffin; and the bearers came to a halt. And He said, 'Young man, I say to you, arise!' The dead man sat up and began to speak. And Jesus gave him back to his mother" (Luke 7:13–15).

111

- When He sensed the needs of the crowd for healing from physical pain and sickness He postponed sitting with His disciples privately in order to minister to the needs of the public: "When He went ashore He saw a large crowd and felt compassion for them and healed their sick" (Matthew 14:14).
- When His disciples were willing to send the crowd off on empty stomachs, Jesus insisted that they be fed. "And they all ate and were satisfied" (Luke 9:12–17)

This is how Jesus expects us to win people for the Kingdom of God. We need to see evangelism as a lifestyle of giving and of engaging with the lost. We must also realize that Christianity is our personal identity rather than our chosen "religion." Once this happens we will be able to see non-Christians (including Muslims) as real people who are loved by God rather than as numbers and evangelistic projects. May the Lord help us be faithful disciples to Him.

> "For we never came with flattering speech, as you know, nor with a pretext for greed—God is witness—nor did we seek glory from men, either from you or from others, even though as apostles of Christ we might have asserted our authority. But we proved to be gentle among you, as a nursing mother tenderly cares for her own children. Having so fond an affection for you, we were well-pleased to impart to you not only the gospel of God but also our own lives, because you had become very dear to us" (I Thessalonians 2:5-8).

Probing Deeper

1. How significant to you are the difficulties and the consequences of reaching Muslims, especially in Muslim countries?

_____

_____

_____

_____

2. In the table of comparisons between Muslim and Western Values, were there any new or strange Muslim values that you were not aware of? If so, share your reaction.

_____

_____

_____

_____

3. Make a list of Muslims you know, and how you can take the first steps to building a relationship of trust and friendship. Start praying for these Muslims with your prayer group.

_____

_____

_____

_____

4. How often do you make a point of ministering to others with hospitality? Are you able to open your home to those God puts on your heart to reach with the Good News? How can you, as an individual or with your family, work on becoming more generous and hospitable?

_____

_____

_____

_____

5. How do you spend your leisure time as an individual and as a family? Is part of that time invested in changing people's lives and in helping others? If not, write some possible ways you can start being Jesus' hands and feet in your community.

_____

_____

_____

_____

Rest on the Road

It is not easy to follow Jesus' example in service and in hospitality if you are depending solely on your own efforts and resources. Use this space to ask God to give you the strength, wisdom, and love to be able to follow His footsteps faithfully and diligently.

_____

_____

_____

_____

_____

_____

_____

_____

_____

_____

Points of Interest

Bible Passages

- Read about Boaz, this generous man, in Ruth 2-4

- Read about Abraham and the three visitors in Genesis 18

Books

- Pippert, Rebecca Manley. *Out of the Saltshaker and Into the World.* InterVarsity Press (1999)

- Hoskins, Edward J. *A Muslim's Heart: What Every Christian Needs to Know to Share Christ with Muslims.* Dawson Media (2003)

Lesson 10

Loving Muslims

Building Spiritual Bridges

Building Spiritual Bridges with Muslims

Part I: A Muslim's Spiritual Life

You might not know that a Muslim's view of religion in relation to life is very different from that of the westerner. If we Christians can begin to understand this, it might be easier for us to approach Muslims and start a conversation about religious beliefs. Religion is one part of the westerner's life, while to a Muslim religion is life itself.

For most westerners, religion:

- Is a private and personal matter
- Is not discussed except among their close circle of family and friends

For a true Christ follower their faith:

- Is a personal choice and not an inherited trait
- Is a growing relationship with the Creator
- Is a response to God's love
- Brings freedom, joy, love, and peace

For a Muslim, religion:

- Is a public affair, and the community has the right to make sure that the person is following Islam
- Is a subject that comes up in everyday conversations, practices, and events
- Requires accountability to the head of the family, the Imam in the Mosque and even to the government
- Is a set of rules and practices that must be performed to please Allah
- Does not involve a personal relationship with the Creator
- Is a necessary submission to Allah out of fear of his wrath
- Means a constant doubt of whether the Muslim has done enough, with no assurance of eternal bliss.
- Is received by birth. According to Islam, "born a Muslim, is always a Muslim", with no right to convert or even consider choosing another religion or faith.

These are the main differences, and it is these key elements of the Muslims' religion that make it difficult for them to understand that there is a better way

and a better life. Thankfully, once the Holy Spirit works in the Muslim's heart, bringing light and saving grace, the Muslim is able to turn to the true God and receive forgiveness, freedom, and joy.

Part II: Keys to Building Spiritual Bridges

Here are ten helpful ideas for you to keep in mind when presenting the Gospel to a Muslim:

1. Use the Word of God

Muslims respect the Bible as a book revealed by God. Learn to quote or read the Bible when speaking with a Muslim and allow it to speak through you to them concerning the issues in question. Encourage your Muslim friend to read the Bible, starting with the Gospel of Luke because it includes the full story of Jesus. Then recommend that they move on to John and then to Romans. Also encourage your friend to read the Psalms, because that book will help teach him or her how to converse with God. Some Muslims may not even want to touch the Bible, believing that it is corrupted. You will learn how to confidently overcome this obstacle in another lesson.

2. Be constantly in prayer

Remember that it is not you personally, but the Holy Spirit who draws people to Christ. Therefore, pray for your Muslim friend before your meeting or visit, pray while you are sharing, and continue to pray later. Witnessing to a Muslim is often accompanied with spiritual warfare and you might experience problems or difficulties as a result. It is advisable to have several believers join you in prayer to defeat the enemy's attempts to distract you from your goal with tribulations. Also, remember that answered prayer is one of the most influential factors in a Muslim's coming to Christ. Ask your Muslim friend if you can pray for him or her and then do it faithfully. Expect an answer from God and watch His power work in your Muslim friend.

3. Be genuine

It often takes many conversations for a Muslim to begin to understand Christianity. Therefore you need to be ready to search, study the Bible, and commit some time to your Muslim friend. If you do not know the answer to one of the questions, do not make one up. Be humbly truthful and promise to find the answer and bring it with you the next time you meet. As you build your relationship, your friend will be watching you and observing how you are living your life. Your Christian principles, lived out on a daily basis, are more important to a Muslim than all the words you could ever say. Reflect Jesus

Christ to your Muslim friend in both act and word.

4. Ask thought-provoking questions

Muslims, like most people, often respond and learn better when asked questions rather than when they are given or told the information. Ask questions like: How can a person receive God's approval? How can I know for sure that I am forgiven? Who is this God I worship, do I know Him personally? Thought-provoking questions will prepare the Muslim to understand your message.

5. Listen attentively

The Muslim will take you seriously after you have listened to him or to her carefully. Make sure you know where the Muslim is spiritually. Is he well read in Islam? Does she pray every day? Is she satisfied or disappointed with her faith? When the Muslim feels that he has been heard, he will be inclined to listen to you as well. Communication needs to function in both directions and you can learn a lot from your Muslim friend if you take the time to listen.

6. Present your beliefs openly

Muslims expect us to express what we believe and they respect people who are religious. Do not be afraid to share what you believe openly, respectfully, and clearly.

7. Do not argue

Many Muslims come from cultures where reason is not the primary factor in determining what truth is. Therefore, reason can sometimes have a limited role in convincing a Muslim. Avoid needless and self-fulfilling arguments. You might win the battle of words, but you will definitely lose the Muslim. Some things can never be resolved through argument or debate, the best thing to remember is that in everything you say, be patient, loving, and peaceful.

8. Never belittle Muhammad or the Qur'an

Muslims all over the world model themselves after their prophet Muhammad. An insult to Muhammad is automatically an insult to them. The Qur'an is a holy book for them and they are ready to die in defense of its authenticity. Be careful and do not speak disrespectfully about the Qur'an or Muhammad. If you are specifically asked about your view of Muhammad and the Qur'an you can answer by saying "I understand that Muhammad is your prophet and the Qur'an is your holy book, but as you know I am a Christian. The Bible is my holy Book and Jesus Christ is my Lord and Savior."

9. Avoid politics

Muslims cannot separate religion and politics. If you allow them to draw you into a political conversation, you will lose them if you do not agree completely with their views. Issues such as the relationship between Palestine and Israel are very sensitive subjects. If questioned on these subjects, be neutral and let them know that you belong to a different, better Kingdom. Turn the conversation away from the physical turmoil here on earth and towards your assurance of heaven.

10. Offer them the Truth with love

Do not be misled by their belief in Jesus or the Bible. Normally these beliefs have a Muslim context and not a biblical one, and in most cases what they know about Jesus and the Bible is limited to what their leaders tell them. Use direct quotes or messages from the Word of God, and if necessary the Qur'an, to help them find the Truth. Make sure that you do all this with the love and compassion that God is able to pour into your heart for the Muslims if you only ask Him to.

Answers from the Word of God

Side Trip: Tell Your Story

Your own testimony might be the most effective story that the Muslim will hear from you because it details the beginning of your personal relationship with God. If you have never written down your testimony, use these questions to help you form an outline. This exercise will be the first step in building a full version; you will have a chance in a following lesson to include more details.

Outline Questions	Your outline—one or two sentences
What is your religious background?	
When did you start to feel the need for God in your life?	
Who was influential in your spiritual journey?	
What Bible passage or passages were most life-changing for you?	
When was the turning point in your relationship with God?	

Main Trip: A Witness to Jesus

Bible Study Passage
Acts 2:22-36

"But Peter, taking his stand with the eleven, raised his voice and declared to them: "Men of Israel, listen to these words: Jesus the Nazarene, a man attested to you by God with miracles and wonders and signs which God performed through Him in your midst, just as you yourselves know— this Man, delivered over by the predetermined plan and foreknowledge

of God, you nailed to a cross by the hands of godless men and put Him to death. But God raised Him up again, putting an end to the agony of death, since it was impossible for Him to be held in its power. For David says of Him… 'You will not abandon my soul to Hades, nor allow your holy one to undergo decay. You have made known to me the ways of life; you will make me full of gladness with your presence.' Brethren, I may confidently say to you regarding the patriarch David that he both died and was buried, and his tomb is with us to this day. And so, because he was a prophet and knew that God had sworn to him with an oath to seat one of his descendants on his throne, he looked ahead and spoke of the resurrection of the Christ, that He was neither abandoned to Hades, nor did His flesh suffer decay. This Jesus God raised up again, to which we are all witnesses. Therefore having been exalted to the right hand of God, and having received from the Father the promise of the Holy Spirit, He has poured forth this which you both see and hear… Therefore let all the house of Israel know for certain that God has made Him both Lord and Christ—this Jesus whom you crucified."

Tell the Facts

This passage from Peter's sermon on Pentecost serves as a model to this day for preaching the gospel and for witnessing. The focus of Peter's sermon is not on current events, church politics, or what physical works please God most. Instead, the focus is on Jesus of Nazareth and on telling the facts about Him; Peter even uses the Old Testament to show the foreshadowing of Jesus. Through the miracles and signs that Jesus performed during His lifetime, God showed the world the credentials of His Son. Central to Peter's message is the fact that "This Jesus God raised up again, to which we are all witnesses" (Acts 2:32). This is the center of our message: The resurrection of Jesus and His victory over death. It means that Jesus is "exalted to the right hand of God" (Acts 2:33) and must be confessed as both Lord and Christ (Acts 2:36).

The message of the Gospel is that simple. God sent His Son to die on the cross in our place, to pay the price for our sins. He rose on the third day victorious over death, to give us eternal life. Are you ready to share that story?

Overcome your Fear

Witnessing to others about Jesus is often accompanied by some kind of fear. It could be fear of criticism by others, fear of rejection, fear of losing the friend, fear of not being able to explain the Gospel correctly. It is encouraging for us to know that Paul himself did not approach his ministry without some fear. In his letter to the church of Corinth he admitted his weakness.

"And when I came to you, brethren, I did not come with superiority of speech or of wisdom, proclaiming to you the testimony of God. For I determined to know nothing among you except Jesus Christ, and Him crucified. I was with you in weakness and in fear and in much trembling, and my message and my preaching were not in persuasive words of wisdom, but in demonstration of the Spirit and of power, so that your faith would not rest on the wisdom of men, but on the power of God" (I Corinthians 2:1–5).

Again, in Ephesians, Paul pleads to the church by saying: "… and pray on my behalf, that utterance may be given to me in the opening of my mouth, to make known with boldness the mystery of the gospel, for which I am an ambassador in chains; that in proclaiming it I may speak boldly, as I ought to speak" (Ephesians 6:19–20).

The fear of witnessing is the same today as it was during the times of Paul and the first disciples. God knows that we will struggle in this area but He promises to come to our aid if we call upon Him to help us.

"He will call upon Me, and I will answer him; I will be with him in trouble; I will rescue him and honor him" (Psalm 91:15).

"I sought the Lord, and He answered me, and delivered me from all my fears" (Psalm 34:4).

The amazing thing is that God calls and uses all personality types and styles in His service. He is more concerned about our attitudes and motives than our abilities and skills. God does not expect all of us to be biblical scholars or eloquent speakers, but He does expect us to love and to learn His Word. When we are obedient in this area God will bless our efforts and help us overcome our fear of witnessing. It is important to know that though we may stumble in our words, God will bless us for our efforts. Proverbs 29:25 tells us: "The fear of man brings a snare, but he who trusts in the Lord will be exalted." We can overcome our fear of witnessing by knowing the Word of God and by depending on Him to come to our rescue when that fear strikes.

False Tolerance

Satan is exploiting the word tolerance these days to stop us from boldly witnessing to others. We hear comments such as these circulating among the followers of Christ: "I don't want to offend my friend, so I really cannot tell her that Jesus is the *only* way to God," or, "They will accuse me of being intolerant if I share my belief that the Bible is the *only* Word of God" or, "I cannot stand up and declare that this is not right without being accused of being intolerant."

DARE *TO* EXPLORE

In the past, tolerance meant that other people had the right to express their opinions without being condemned. Tolerance meant we accepted other people as they were, though we may differ in our beliefs and opinions. However, tolerance today has come to mean something radically different. This new type of tolerance means never saying that someone else is wrong and never expressing any belief that might offend another person. If someone expresses an opposing view, they are considered intolerant and prejudiced. This kind of tolerance is an evil method to silence the truth. Being intolerant does not mean being unloving or hateful towards other people.

To a Christian, intolerance should be standing against sin, against deviating from or twisting the truth, and against anything that comes from Satan, but certainly not against people. Jesus did not tolerate sin, on the contrary, He spoke in love, correcting others and declaring the truth. Jesus loved the sinner but hated the sin, and this is the example we must follow. We are called to proclaim the truth with a humble heart and a loving spirit, seeking the guidance of the Holy Spirit.

> "If you are insulted because of the name of Christ, you are blessed, for the Spirit of glory and of God rests on you. If you suffer, it should not be as a murderer or thief or any other kind of criminal, or even as a meddler. However, if you suffer as a Christian, do not be ashamed, but praise God that you bear that name" (I Peter 14-16, NIV).

Use a Simple Presentation of the Gospel

You may be saying to yourself, "I know that I need to witness, but what exactly do I say? How do I sum up the 66 books of the Bible, 2,000 years of church history, and thousands of volumes of theology?" You don't have to be a scholar to witness to a Muslim.

Here is one way you can simply present the Gospel message to your Muslim friend. Some people refer to this method as the "Roman Road," and it is divided into four parts.

1. All men are sinners: you, me, everyone

It is written, "There is none righteous, not even one; there is none who understands, there is none who seeks for God; all have turned aside, together they have become useless; there is none who does good, there is not even one" (Romans 3:10-12).

"All have sinned and fall short of the glory of God" (Romans 3:23).

The first step is to understand that we are all sinners; we were all born with sin and we all continue to sin. Where did this sin come from? Read Genesis

2:4-3:24, which talks about the original sin and how it led to our separation from God. When using this passage in evangelism, be sure to emphasize God's promise to send a Savior, first mentioned in Genesis 3:15.

2. Sin has a price

> "For the wages of sin is death" (Romans 6:23a).

Sin has a price – death. We all die physically as a result of original sin, but the ultimate death is the spiritual death which separates us from God, and which will last for all eternity. The Bible teaches that there is a place called the Lake of Fire where lost people will be in torment forever (Revelation 20:14). It is the place where people who are spiritually dead will remain. Just as vital as understanding that we are all sinners is understanding that we all deserve death for our sin.

3. Jesus paid the price for our sin

> "... but the free gift of God is eternal life in Christ Jesus our Lord" (Romans 6:23b).

Salvation is a free gift from God to you! You cannot buy salvation or earn your way to heaven. Jesus, the only sinless man, had the sin of the world placed on Him; He died on the cross and paid the price in our place. No one else could have paid that high price to redeem us except Jesus, who was blameless before the Holy God. "But God demonstrates His own love toward us, in that while we were yet sinners, Christ died for us" (Romans 5:8). But on the third day after His death He rose from the dead as the victor over death (Luke 24:1-7), therefore, He is the only one who can forgive sins.

> "For God so loved the world that He gave His only begotten Son, that whoever believes in Him shall not perish, but have eternal life" (John 3:16).

4. Jesus' work on the Cross must be received by an act of faith

> "... if you confess with your mouth Jesus as Lord, and believe in your heart that God raised Him from the dead, you will be saved; for with the heart a person believes, resulting in righteousness, and with the mouth he confesses, resulting in salvation" (Romans 10:9-10).

To confess means to openly declare your faith to others. Confess to God, to yourself, to other people, "Jesus is Lord." After you confess, repent of your old sinful ways, and allow Jesus to be your King and your Master. Believe in your heart with everything that you are, that Jesus died to take the punishment for

your sin, and that He conquered death. Believe that God raised Jesus from the dead and now that Jesus lives, we can live with him forever. Listen to what Jesus says about confessing and believing: "Therefore everyone who confesses Me before men, I will also confess him before My Father who is in heaven" (Matthew 10:32).

Jesus is eagerly waiting for you to take this step and confess your faith in him. "Behold, I stand at the door and knock; if anyone hears My voice and opens the door, I will come in to him and will dine with him, and he with Me" (Revelation 3:20).

Building spiritual bridges with your Muslim friend does not have to be complicated. Yes, it is important for you to understand the Muslim's spiritual background, but more important is for you yourself to know Jesus personally and to know God's Word. Although connecting with Muslims may be a fearful task for you, it is one that the Holy Spirit will guide you through if you have a willing heart.

Probing Deeper

1. Have you ever hesitated in approaching a Muslim neighbor or co-worker because you did not understand the differences between Christianity and Islam?

   _____

   _____

   _____

   _____

2. "Born a Muslim, always a Muslim." What is your response to this phrase that Muslims use?

   _____

   _____

   _____

   _____

3. What are some differences in the ways that you view religion, compared to the ways a Muslim does?

   _____

   _____

   _____

   _____

   _____

4. Do you remember how you understood salvation through Jesus Christ for the first time?

   _____

   _____

   _____

   _____

   _____

5. How much space in your life do you allow your faith to fill?

_____

_____

_____

_____

_____

Rest on the Road

Fears about sharing your faith are very common. What are you most afraid of? Ask God to help you overcome those fears and to open new opportunities for you to witness.

_____

_____

_____

_____

_____

_____

_____

_____

_____

_____

_____

Points of Interest

Bible Passages

- Acts 4 and 7

Books

- McDowell, Josh. *More than a Carpenter.* Living Books, (1987)

- Tanagho, Samy. *Glad News! God Loves you My Muslim Friend.* Authentic Media, (2004)

Web Sites

- http://www.livingwaters.com/witnessingtool/browse.shtml#indepth (accessed April 2014)

Lesson 11

Apologetics

The Bible and The Triune God

Part I: The Bible

Corruption of the Bible

One of the biggest hurdles to overcome when witnessing to Muslims is their belief that the Bible is a corrupted book. Muslims have been taught by their leaders that the Bible has been changed by man and therefore is no longer authoritative. How would you address this question?

A good way to start the discussion is by asking the Muslim: "When do you think the Bible was corrupted, before the time of the Qur'an, or after?"

Before the time of the Qur'an

If the Muslim answers that the Bible was corrupted before the time of the Qur'an, ask: "Why then does the Qur'an instruct Muslims to acknowledge both the Torah and the Ingil (the Gospel)?" Use these verses from the Qur'an to prove your point:

> "It was We who revealed the Torah to Moses. Therein was guidance and light. By its standard have been judged the Jews, by the prophets who bowed to Allah's will by the rabbis and the doctors of Law, for to them was entrusted the protection of Allah's book and they were witnesses to thereto" (Sura 5:44).

> "And in their footsteps we sent Isa the son of Mary, confirming the Law that had come before him. We sent him the Gospel therein was guidance and light and confirmation of the Law that had come before him. A guidance and an admonition to those who fear Allah" (Sura 5:46).

From these two verses we see that the Qur'an acknowledges that Allah proclaimed the Torah to be guidance and light for his people, and that Allah sent Isa (Jesus) to confirm the Law that came before him. The Qur'an also considers the Gospel to be guidance and light, and whoever fails to believe in the Torah and the Gospel is considered a rebel. In historical perspective this means that according to the Qur'an, the Torah and the Gospel were still authoritative texts, uncorrupted by man, at approximately AD 624 when the Qur'an was being revealed to Muhammad. Therefore, a Muslim who claims that the Bible was corrupted before the Qur'an was revealed needs to examine closely what the Qur'an says about the Bible and not build his or her beliefs on oral traditions and the various opinions of Muslim leaders.

After the time of the Qur'an

The Muslim might say that the Bible was corrupted after the sixth century AD. How would you respond to that claim?

By the sixth century, the Bible had been translated into many languages including Latin, Armenian, Syriac, Coptic, Ethiopic, Aramaic, and Greek.[1] Copies of these translations circulated widely in Asia, North Africa, and Europe. The Torah was already present among the Jews in Hebrew, and in Greek and Aramaic translation. Both Old and New Testament were in wide circulation among Christians. Imagine someone trying to gather all the copies and translations from all of these continents, and then attempting to create a new original version of the Bible; that would be impossible! It is clear that the Bible could not have been corrupted after the time of the Qur'an.

The evidence for the reliability of the Bible[2]

The Bible, both Old and New Testament, was preserved and transmitted by communities who held the text to be sacred. Sacred texts are not typically handled in a loose way by any religious community. Both Old and New Testament specifically command that God's Word is not to be altered in any way. For example, in Deuteronomy 4:2 God says, "You shall not add to the word which I am commanding you, nor take away from it, that you may keep the commandments of the Lord your God which I command you." Or again, in Deuteronomy 12:32, "Whatever I command you, you shall be careful to do; you shall not add to nor take away from it." The final paragraph of the Bible in Revelation 22:18-19 says, "I testify to everyone who hears the words of the prophecy of this book: if anyone adds to them, God will add to him the plagues which are written in this book; and if anyone takes away from the words of the book of this prophecy, God will take away his part from the tree of life and from the holy city, which are written in this book."

The actual text of the Bible was transmitted by communities of scribes who dedicated their lives to the accurate preservation of the text.

In the Old Testament, most manuscripts have scribal notations at the end of each major section indicating the accuracy of the text. The note at the end of Deuteronomy, for example, says that the total number of verses in the Torah is 5,845, the total number of paragraphs is 167, and the total number of words is 79,856, and the total number of letters is 400, 945!

For the New Testament, there is a super-abundance of manuscript evidence to establish with certainty the New Testament text. There are more than 5000 Greek manuscripts and 10,000 early Latin manuscripts. Some of these are entire copies. Several of these manuscripts date from the first generations after

---

[1]*The History of Christianity Vol. I*, Kenneth Scott Latourette.

[2]*The New Testament Speaks*, Glenn W. Barker, William L. Lane, J. Ramsey Michaels (Harper & Row, 1969).

the death and resurrection of Jesus. By way of comparison, there are only eight manuscripts of the Greek historian Herodotus which date from 1,300 years after the date of composition. There are only twenty copies of Livy's Roman history which date from 900 years after the author's own time.

Especially in the past 150 years, the manuscripts of both the Old and New Testament have been rigorously studied and published by international scholars from a variety of backgrounds. The results of this scholarly research bears weight to the statement that the Bible is the best attested and preserved document of the ancient world.

Who corrupted the Bible?

After overcoming the obstacle of when the Bible was corrupted, the next question to ask the Muslim is: "Who do you think corrupted the Bible, the Jews or the Christians?" Try to help the Muslim think through this reasonably.

If the Jews had tried to make changes to the Bible, wouldn't they have made changes to serve their own interest? The Old Testament is full of stories about kings and leaders who turned away from God, worshipped idols, and committed shameful sins. Why didn't the Jews keep the good stories that would glorify their past and omit the less flattering events in their history? Additionally, in the New Testament, why didn't the Jews omit all of what Jesus accused them of and why didn't they change their position of responsibility and cruelty in the crucifixion story? If the Jews tried to change any part of the Bible, wouldn't the Christians have made a stand against changing the revered Word of God? Aside from this argument, historical records are a reference that would deter anyone trying to rewrite a series of events.

The same reasoning applies to the accusation that Christians corrupted the Bible. Why would the Christians corrupt the Old Testament when it includes hundreds of prophecies about the coming of Jesus? Why would they change the New Testament when thousands of them were killed in the first century because they refused to abandon the very Gospel they are supposedly guilty of changing.

You can close your discussion by gently pointing out that according to the Qur'an, Allah is all-powerful. If He is all-powerful therefore he should be able to protect the Bible, His own revelation, from corruption.

Reading the Bible

At this point you can ask the Muslim whether she or he will accept a copy of the Bible to read. Advise the Muslim to start reading in the following order:

- The Gospel of Luke, because it tells the full story of Jesus' life.

- The Gospel of John, which reveals the love of God to the world through Jesus Christ, His Word.
- The book of Acts, where the message of Christ continues.
- The letter to the Romans, where salvation by grace is fully explained.

Muslims believe in the validity of the prophet David and that he wrote the book of Psalms. Encourage the Muslim to meditate on the Psalms while reading the other books. This will help him or her learn how to speak to God and have an intimate relationship with the Creator. Invite the Muslim to call out to God each time he reads the Bible by saying "God, please show me the true way and reveal yourself to me."

Part II: The Triune God

Muslims consider their religion to be superior to all others because of its monotheistic tenets. They accuse Christians of blasphemy because of their false assumption that Christians worship three gods. Mohammad incorrectly taught in the Qur'an that the Trinity consisted of God, Mary, and Jesus. Even today when corrected by Christians, Muslims continue to oppose the Triune God; the Father, the Son, and the Holy Spirit.

> *"O People of the Book! Commit no excesses in your religion: Nor say of Allah aught but the truth... Say not "Trinity": desist: it will be better for you: for Allah is one Allah." (Sura 4:171).*

Explaining the Triune God

When discussing this subject it is very important to warmly assure the Muslim that you do believe in one God. You also need to confirm that the doctrine of the triune God is crucial to the Christian faith. The Father, the Son, and the Holy Spirit are all to be worshiped and glorified equally as the Triune God. The perfect love and unity of the triune God is a model of the oneness and affection that characterizes our Christian relationships in the Body of Christ. At the same time, the doctrine of the Triune God is one that is divine and not human.

The word **Trinity** never appears in the Bible. Therefore, it would be better to use the term **Triune God.**

There are several important things to remember when discussing the Triune God with the Muslim:

1. God is an undivided one. Monotheism is the heart of the Christian faith.
2. The Deity of each of the three persons, Father, Son, and Holy Spirit, must be affirmed as being qualitatively the same; the Son is God, the Father is

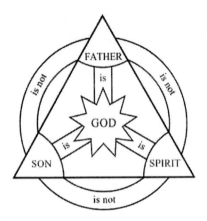

God, and the Holy Spirit is God. The three persons share the same essence or being. The one God exists in the distinct and co-equal entities of the Father, the Son, and the Holy Spirit. They fully share divine attributes such as, holiness, omnipotence, omnipresence, grace, love, etc.

3. God is three persons simultaneously and continuously. God does not manifest Himself as one part of the Triune God and give up being the other parts. The Triune God is eternal.

4. He has always been three; Father, Son, and Holy Spirit, and all of the three have always been divine.

5. The function of one member of the Triune God may for a time be subordinate to one or both of the other members, but that does not imply any inferiority of essence. Each of the three parts of the Triune God has had, for a period of time, a particular function unique to Himself. These are temporary roles to accomplish a specific end. The Son did not become less than the Father during His earthly incarnation but He did submit to the will of the Father. In the same way the Holy Spirit is submissive to the ministry of the Son (John chapter 14-16) as well as to the will of the Father, but He is not less than they are.[3]

There are many verses in the Bible that explain the nature of the Triune God. Here are some Bible verses you may use to support your argument:

- **There is only one God**

  "Hear, O Israel! The Lord is our God, the Lord is one!" (Deuteronomy 6:4).

  "The scribe said to Him, 'Right, Teacher; You have truly stated that He is one, and there is no one else beside Him'" (Mark 12:32).

- **God is a Triune God**

  "Go therefore and make disciples of all the nations, baptizing them in the name of the Father and the Son and the Holy Spirit" (Matthew 28:19).

  "But when the fullness of the time came, **God** sent forth **His Son,** born of a woman, born under the Law, so that He might redeem those who were under the Law, that we might receive the adoption as sons. Because you are sons, God has sent forth the **Spirit** of His Son into our hearts, crying, 'Abba! **Father!**'" (Galatians 4:4-6).

The following chart gives you more biblical resources to use when discussing the divinity of the Triune God.

---

[3]Millard J. Erickson, *Christian Theology* (Grand Rapids: Baker Book House, 1985).

Characteristic	The Father	The Son	The Holy Spirit
The Creator	Genesis 1:1	Colossians 1:16-17	Genesis 1:2
The Unchanging and Eternal One	Isaiah 43:10	Micah 5:2	Hebrews 9:114
The One Called God	Ephesians 4:6	John 1:1-5	II Corinthians 3:15-17
The Omnipotent One	Nahum 1:3–6	John 16:15	Luke 1:35
The All-Knowing One	Psalm 139:1-3	Luke 5:22	I Corinthians 2:10-11

Illustrations

To simplify the concept of the Triune God, you can offer some illustrations to help the Muslim understand it. Although our infinite God cannot be described by finite illustrations, these explanations do help in processing the information in our human minds. Do no hesitate to use physical examples with Muslims; remember that Jesus used parables to explain complicated Kingdom truths to His disciples. Here are some common illustrations:

- A man can be a son, a husband, and a father at the same time, but he is only one person.
- The one chemical substance of H_2O (water) is always present in three different forms; solid, liquid, and vapor.
- We experience the sun in three forms, we can see its shape, it gives us light,and we can feel its heat.
- A person is made of body, soul, and spirit, but he is one person.

The Muslim might ask, "Doesn't $1 + 1 + 1 = 3$?" But the truth is that God who is the Father, the Son, and the Holy Spirit is infinite, so if we add infinity + infinity + infinity the result is still infinity. Considering that infinity is an incomprehensible mystery, so is the understanding of the Triune God ultimately beyond human understanding. Belief in the Triune God is not irrational, but trans-rational: that is, it is above our human minds to understand.

> "For now we see in a mirror dimly, but then face to face; now I know in part, but then I will know fully just as I also have been fully known" (1 Corinthians 13:12).

The Saving Grace of the Triune God

The Bible says that "For God so loved the world that He gave His only begotten Son that whoever believes in Him shall not perish but have everlasting life" (John 3:16). Thus we see that the Father loves man and wants his salvation, and the Son willingly paid the price to attain that salvation. The Holy Spirit awakens man's conscience and convicts him of his sins (John 16:7–8), so that he can receive Christ as the Savior. There is no salvation except that which is offered by God—the Father, the Son and the Holy Spirit—the only true and living God.

Remember

In addition to helping the Muslim overcome general misconceptions about the Bible and the Triune God through discussion, remember that praying for the Muslim is an essential part of this process. Only God through the Holy Spirit and His Living Word can break down the walls of resistance, ignorance, and blind submission to Islam. Do not be discouraged if you feel ineffective, allow God to work in your Muslim friend's heart.

Probing Deeper

1. In your own words, write how you can explain to a Muslim that the Bible was still intact before Muhammad's time.

_____

_____

_____

_____

2. Why is it unlikely that the Bible was corrupted after the sixth century AD? Explain.

_____

_____

_____

_____

3. Give some physical illustrations you can use to explain to the Muslim how God can be three in one.

_____

_____

_____

_____

_____

4. What are some divine characteristics that the Father, the Son, and the Holy Spirit share in addition to the ones listed in the chart under "God is a Triune God"?

_____

_____

_____

_____

_____

5. How does your understanding of the relationship between the Father, the Son, and the Holy Spirit affect your personal faith?

_____

_____

_____

_____

_____

Rest on the Road

It is not easy to accept a concept which is beyond our human minds, especially when it has to do with our faith and eternal destiny. If you struggle in this area, ask the Almighty God to help you understand and believe. Thank Him for who He is and ask Him to help you in your journey of faith.

_____

_____

_____

_____

_____

_____

_____

_____

_____

_____

_____

Points of Interest

Bible Passages

- Genesis 1-2: the creation story

- Matthew 3:16-17: Jesus' baptism

- John 1

- Luke 22:39-46: Jesus praying in Gethsemane

Books

- Bramsen, P.D. *One God One Message.* Xulon Press (2007)

- Owen, John. *Communion With the Triune God.* Crossway Books (2007)

Web Sites

- Hartman, K. Dayton. *Answering Muslim Objections To The Trinity* http://www.answering-islam.org/authors/hartman/trinity_objections.html (accessed April 2014)

- The Bible http://www.answering-islam.org/Bible/index.html (accessed April 2014)

Lesson 12

Apologetics

Jesus the Son of God and the Crucifixion

Part I: Jesus the Son of God

The phrase "Son of God" is offensive to every Muslim. The idea of God having a son is considered blasphemous. When confronted with this concept, Muslims will often quote this verse from the Qur'an: *"God neither begets nor is begotten"* (Sura 112:3). Why is the Son-ship of Jesus an affront to the Muslim faith, and how do we help them understand the true meaning of this integral part of the Christian faith?

There are two basic misunderstandings that lead Muslims to reject Jesus as the Son of God. They think that Jesus was either a human who became God, and/or that Jesus came as the result of a physical relationship between God and Mary.

Muslim Misperception: Jesus was human who became a god

Muslims react to the concept of Jesus as the son of God, as blasphemy. They think Christians believe that Jesus was a human who became God. *"And when Allah will say: O Isa son of Maryam! did you say to men, Take me and my mother for two gods besides Allah he will say: Glory be to Thee, it did not befit me that I should say what I had no right to (say); if I had said it, Thou wouldst indeed have known it...."* (Sura 5:116).

We must explain to the Muslim quite clearly that:

- **Jesus is not a man that became God but God became man through Jesus Christ.** "By common confession, great is the mystery of godliness: He who was revealed in the flesh, was vindicated in the Spirit, Seen by angels, Proclaimed among the nations, Believed on in the world, Taken up in glory" (I Timothy 3:16).
- **God did not give up being God in order to become man in the form of Jesus.** When Jesus was on earth God continued to be omnipresent, He was still everywhere else. God spoke from heaven when Jesus was in the flesh:

  "And He was transfigured before them; and His face shone like the sun, and His garments became as white as light... and behold, a voice out of the cloud said, "This is My beloved Son, with whom I am well-pleased; listen to Him!" (Matthew 17:2-5).

It is important to confirm to the Muslim that Jesus was there before the beginning of time and that He appeared in the flesh at a certain historical time. "In the beginning was the Word, and the Word was with God, and the Word was God. He was in the beginning with God" (John 1:1–2).

Muslim misperception: Jesus was born as the result of a physical union between God and Mary

Muhammad misunderstood what the term "Son of God" meant with respect to Christianity. He thought of "Son" only in terms of sexual reproduction, and concluded that God fathered a child with Mary. Believing that no holy being could be the result of a physical union, he denounced this biblical belief. Muhammad was unable to distinguish between Jesus as the Son of God, and the Arab Pagan belief; that idols were the offspring of gods. In the sixth century there were three main idols in Mecca that were worshipped: Al-Lat, Al-Uzza, and Manat. They were known as daughters of the supreme pagan god Hubal—or Allah. Muhammad thought that Christians related to Jesus—the Son of God—in the same way the Arab Pagans understood their idols. This is the reasoning behind the Qur'an's Sura 9:30 *"The Christians say the Messiah is the Son of God, that is a saying from their mouths."*

We must confirm to the Muslim that we reject the idea that God had a physical relationship with Mary. We believe that the eternal Son of God is one with the Father from all eternity, united to Him in one Spirit. "… The 'Father-Son' relationship between God the Father and Jesus Christ, is achieved by the gracious choice of the Father and the faithful obedience and service of the Son, and not by creation and certainly not by procreation."[1]

What does it mean to be the Son of God?

Once the Muslim understands that Jesus is not the result of a marriage, and He is not a man who became a god, the next logical question for the Muslim to ask is "Why then is Jesus called the Son of God?"

First we have to explain that the expression "Son of God" is an analogical term. It indicates origin, a close association or identification. In Christian theology it describes the relationship of two persons of the triune God. It expresses an intimate relationship between these two Persons: God the Father and God the Son—Jesus the Messiah. Give the Muslim this example: In Egypt, Egyptians call themselves sons and daughters of the Nile. Does this mean that the Nile got married and had children? God chose to describe the relationship between Himself and Jesus as a father-son relationship because it is a term we can understand and relate to. But in truth the father-son relationship between God the Father and God the Son is much stronger and deeper than we can comprehend.

---

[1]Hahn, Ernest and Engelbrecht, Luther, "Jesus as the Son of God." answering-islam. 19 November 2009 http://www.answering-islam.org/Hahn/son.html (accessed April 2014).

Second, we need to emphasize that the language "Son of God" is used to describe the Messiah as a royal son, who rules with His Father. "For a child will be born to us, a son will be given to us; And the government will rest on His shoulders; And His name will be called Wonderful Counselor, Mighty God, Eternal Father, Prince of Peace" (Isaiah 9:6).

Part II: The Crucifixion

What Muslims believe

Muslims have different beliefs about the crucifixion. The three main beliefs are derived from these Qur'anic verses:

- Sura 4:157-158: *"And their saying: Surely we have killed the Messiah, Isa son of Maryam, the messenger of Allah; and they did not kill him nor did they crucify him, but it appeared to them so (like Isa) and most surely those who differ therein are only in a doubt about it; they have no knowledge respecting it, but only follow a conjecture, and they killed him not for sure. Nay! Allah took him up to Himself; and Allah is Mighty, Wise."*

From this well-used verse, Muslims claim that Isa was not the one who was crucified by the Jews. Allah put the image of Isa on someone else at the time of Isa's crucifixion. Some say it was Judas Iscariot while others claim it was one of the disciples to whom Isa promised paradise if he died in his place. Still others say that it was a Roman soldier named Titawus. From the same verse Muslims believe that Allah took Isa up to paradise and saved Him from the hands of the Jews, and so Allah deceived the Jews in order to save Isa!

- In Sura 19:33, Isa said: *"So peace is on me the day I was born, the day that I die, and the day that I shall be raised up to life."*

From this verse, some Muslims believe that Isa did die naturally at some point and that Allah raised him up and took him to paradise.

- Sura 3:55: *"Behold! Allah said: 'O Isa! I will take thee and raise thee to Myself and clear thee (of the falsehoods) of those who blaspheme; I will make those who follow thee superior to those who reject faith, to the Day of Resurrection: Then shall ye all return unto me, and I will judge between you of the matters wherein ye dispute.'"*

Some Muslims quote this verse to confirm their belief that Isa did not see death, but was raised to the heavens so that the blasphemers would realize that he was truly sent by Allah.

Two other widely-asserted claims:

- The crucifixion did not even happen but was a later story fabricated by Christians.
- Jesus was crucified but did not die; He "swooned" on the cross and later recovered. The "swoon theory" is mainly held by the Ahmadiya sect and the Nation of Islam.

The crucifixion and resurrection of Jesus is the core of our salvation. In I Corinthians 15:3-4, Paul states that he passed on to early believers two matters of utmost significance: "For what I received I passed on to you as of first importance: that Christ died for our sins according to the Scriptures, that he was buried, that he was raised on the third day according to the Scriptures." That is why Satan uses different means to deceive people into believing that Jesus Christ was not crucified. Without the crucifixion and the resurrection, Jesus would be like any other prophet who came before Him or after Him. Again in I Corinthians 15:17-19, Paul writes that "And if Christ has not been raised, your faith is futile; you are still in your sins. Then those also who have fallen asleep in Christ are lost. If only for this life we have hope in Christ, we are of all people most to be pitied." Indeed, "the word of the cross is foolishness to those who are perishing, but to us who are being saved it is the power of God" (I Corinthians 1:18).

Helping the Muslim accept the truth of the crucifixion

It is important to prepare yourself to give evidence of the crucifixion of Jesus Christ when the Muslim asks the question. You don't have to know all the answers, but you can at least direct the Muslim to good and trusted resources. Some Muslims will ask for historical evidence, while others will say that they only accept what the Qur'an states. In either case, here are some main points you can share with your Muslim friend.

Secular Evidence of the Crucifixion

There are at least seventeen ancient texts written by non-Christian historians and witnesses that record the various aspects of Jesus' earthly ministry. Most of these writings originated in the first to the mid-second century. These texts are consistent with information presented in the Bible.

Here are three examples that you may want to use with the Muslim:

1. Flavius Josephus, a Jewish historian (AD 38–100+), wrote about Jesus in his *Jewish Antiquities*. He writes: "Now there was about this time Jesus, a wise man, if it be lawful to call him a man; for he was a doer of wonderful works, a teacher of such men as receive the truth with pleasure. He

drew over to him both many of the Jews and many of the Gentiles. He was [the] Christ. And when Pilate, at the suggestion of the principal men amongst us, had condemned him to the cross, those that loved him at the first did not forsake him; for he appeared to them alive again the third day; as the divine prophets had foretold these and ten thousand other wonderful things concerning him. And the tribe of Christians, so named from him, are not extinct at this day."[2]

2. Cornelius Tacitus (AD 55–120), an historian of first-century Rome, is considered one of the most accurate historians of the ancient world.[3] An excerpt from Tacitus tells us that the Roman emperor Nero "inflicted the most exquisite tortures on a class... called Christians... Christus [Christ], from whom the name had its origin, suffered the extreme penalty during the reign of Tiberius at the hands of one of our procurators, Pontius Pilatus..." (Tacitus, A. 15.44).

3. The Jewish *Talmud*, certainly not biased toward Jesus, concurs with the Bible about the major events of His life. From the Talmud: "On the eve of Passover they hanged Yeshu. And an announcer went out, in front of him, for forty days (saying): 'He is going to be stoned because he practiced sorcery and enticed and led Israel astray. Anyone who knows anything in his favor, let him come and plead in his behalf.' But, not having found anything in his favor, they hanged him on the eve of the Passover."[4]

This is remarkable information considering that most ancient historians focused on the lives of political and military leaders, not on obscure rabbis from distant provinces of the Roman Empire. Yet ancient historians (Jews, Greeks, and Romans), though not believers themselves, confirm the crucifixion event presented in the four Gospels of the New Testament.

What about the Qur'an?

• The Qur'an affirms that the Bible is the preserved Word of God.

• The Bible affirms Jesus' crucifixion.

• The Qur'an denies the crucifixion.

Therefore, the Qur'an contradicts itself: it affirms the preservation and authority of the Bible while denying one of its essential teachings. This lack of continuity prevents men from embracing the cross of Christ for salvation, while trying to establish the Qur'an's credibility by appealing to the Holy Bible as a

---

[2]Flavius Josephus, *The Works of Flavius Josephus* (JOE), trans. William Whiston (Auburn and Buffalo, NY: John E. Beardsley, 1895), BibleWorks, v.18.3.3.

[3]Josh McDowell, *The New Evidence that Demands a Verdict* (Thomas Nelson Publishers, 1999) 55.

[4]Josh McDowell, *He Walked Among Us* (Thomas Nelson Publishers, 1988) 53.

DARE
TO EXPLORE

source. Point your Muslim friend to these verses from the Qur'an to help him or her embrace the Bible in its entirety, including the crucifixion and resurrection of Jesus Christ:

> *"But if you are in doubt as to what We have revealed to you, ask those who read the Book before you…"* (Sura 10:94).

> *"If they had observed the Torah and the Gospel and that which was revealed unto them from their Lord, they would surely have been nourished from above them and from beneath their feet…"* (Sura 5:66).

New Testament fulfillment of Old Testament Prophecies

The New Testament is a valid source of information about Jesus. As a literary document, it provides better material than any other ancient classical writing. The New Testament has far more manuscript portions than any other ancient text concerning the life of Jesus, and the copies have proven much closer to the originals in both accuracy and date. In addition to these facts, no portions of the New Testament books are missing, while large amounts have been lost from other classical works.

We have in the Old Testament over 300 references including 60 major prophecies about a promised redeemer who was to die on the cross and then rise again. In the 1960's, Peter W. Stoner and Robert C. Newman wrote a book entitled *Science Speaks.* The book was based on the science of probability and vouched for by the American Scientific Affiliation. The writers proved that using only 8 of these 60 prophecies, the probability of one man fulfilling all eight is equal to 1 in 10^{17} or 100,000,000,000,000,000.[5] Jesus did not fulfill just 8 of these prophecies; He fulfilled *all* the Old Testament prophecies that foretold His coming![6]

Many Muslims come to believe in Jesus Christ as the only Savior, after they have compared the Old Testament prophecies to their fulfillments in the person of Jesus Christ. Lead the Muslim to the Old Testament Bible passages that point towards Christ and then to the prophecies' fulfillments in the New Testament.

---

[5]Peter W. Stoner, *Science Speaks*, http://sciencespeaks.dstoner.net/Christ_of_Prophecy.html#c9 (accessed April 2014).

[6]It is hard to understand the concept of a number as large as 10^{17}. One way to understand it is to imagine that you have 10^{17} in coins. You mark one of these coins with a special symbol of a royal crown. If you spread them out, they will cover the state of Texas about three feet deep. You send a person to walk around that sea of coins with a blindfold over his eyes. He bends down and selects a coin. When he removes the blindfold and examines the coin; he finds that the first coin he has selected bears the royal crown! This is the possibility of 1 in 10^{17}!

Here is a list of some of the prophecies regarding Jesus, the Messiah[7]:

Event in Jesus' life	Prophecy	Fulfillment
Will come from the seed of David	Psalm 132:11; Isaiah 11:10; Jeremiah 23:5; 33:15	Matthew 1:6; Luke 1:32-33; Acts 2:30; Romans 1:3
Will be born in Bethlehem	Micah 5:2	Matthew 2:1; Luke 2:4-6
Will be born of a virgin	Isaiah 7:14	Matthew 1:18-25; Luke 1:26-35
Galilee will be the first area of His ministry	Isaiah 9:1-8	Matthew 4:12-16
Will perform miracles	Isaiah 35:5-6	Matthew 11:3-6; John 11:47
Will enter Jerusalem on a donkey	Zechariah 9:9	Matthew 21:1-10
Will be crucified	Psalm 22; Psalm 69:21	Matthew 27:34-50; John 19:28-30
Will be pierced	Zechariah 12:10; Psalm 22:16	John 19:34, 37
No bone will be broken	Psalm 34:20	John 19:36
Will be resurrected	Isaiah 25:8	John 20; I Corinthians 15:54
Will ascend to heaven	Psalm 68:18	Luke 24:51; Acts 1:9
The crucifixion story	Isaiah 53	Matthew 27:27-56, Mark 15:21-38, Luke 23:26-49, and John 19:16-37

[7]Geisler, N. L. *Baker Encyclopedia of Christian Apologetics Baker reference library* (Baker Books, Grand Rapids, 1999).

As you reach out to your Muslim friend, remember that you are only planting the seed. We cannot stress enough the importance of prayer. Even though you might be able to answer all the Muslim's questions about Christ, the Muslim needs to open his or her heart to the Holy Spirit, so keep praying and never give up.

> "…No one can say, 'Jesus is Lord' except by the Holy Spirit"
> (I Corinthians 12:3)

Probing Deeper

1. What are some false beliefs about Jesus, "the Son of God," that Muslims have been led to accept as true?

   _____

   _____

   _____

   _____

2. If the Muslim asks you: "Why is Jesus called the Son of God?" How can you answer simply and clearly?

   _____

   _____

   _____

   _____

3. Muslims have different beliefs about the crucifixion. List some examples that you read in this lesson and add your comments.

   _____

   _____

   _____

   _____

   _____

4. How can fulfilled Old Testament prophecies lead the Muslim to believe in the Crucifixion and Resurrection of Jesus Christ?

   _____

   _____

   _____

   _____

   _____

5. What are some Bible verses that have been meaningful to you in your understanding of what Jesus did for you on the cross? Be ready to share them with the Muslim.

_____

_____

_____

_____

_____

Rest on the Road

You started to write the outlines of your testimony in Lesson 10. Now is the time to prepare the full version of your salvation story. We encourage you to have it written and ready so that you will be prepared to share it with your Muslim friend. Remember God's commandment: "But in your hearts set apart Christ as Lord. Always be prepared to give an answer to everyone who asks you to give the reason for the hope that you have. But do this with gentleness and respect" (I Peter 3:15, NIV).

_____

_____

_____

_____

_____

_____

_____

_____

_____

_____

_____

Points of Interest

Bible Passages

The Crucifixion and Resurrection Story of our Lord and Savior Jesus Christ:

- Matthew 26:17-28:20
- Mark 14:12-16:8
- Luke 22:1-24:11
- John 13:1-20:31

Books

- Geisler, Normal L. and Saleeb, Abdul. *Answering Islam.* Baker Book House (1993)
- McDowell, Josh. *The New Evidence that Demands a Verdict.* Thomas Nelson (1999)

Web Sites

- The "Shame of the Cross" and its Glory http://www.answering-islam.org/Cross/index.html (accessed April 2014)

Final Thoughts

Usually when we end a trip we keep memories of our experiences tucked away in our minds. Sometimes we keep pictures or videos we can return to in order to remind us of a time in the past. We go back and reflect on where we've been and what we did with friends and family.

Our desire is that this study will not be stored away as a memory for later, but will spur you on to continue your journey of evangelism. We hope that what you learned will be dynamic, and will produce a fruitful crop not only in you and your study group, but also in the lives of the Muslims in your neighborhood and in your community.

We hope you'll consider this trip as a first step in a life-long journey of exploring ways to love Muslims and build bridges of friendship and trust with them. You didn't take this journey by coincidence, maybe God is calling you to serve among Muslims here or abroad. Or perhaps God is calling you to raise awareness in your community about Islam and how to differentiate between Islam and Muslims. It may be that God is preparing you now so you will be ready when a Muslim family moves in next door.

We encourage you to make plans with your group in the coming weeks to meet Muslims and continue the journey that you began with this study. If you would like to know where there are Muslims in your area, go to www.calloflove.org and look under Free Resources. We as a ministry are always available to answer your questions, provide you with materials and help you in your outreach events. Most importantly we are available to pray with you.

We pray that the Lord will empower, encourage, and give you the wisdom you need to continue this journey.

"Now to Him who is able to do far more abundantly beyond all that we ask or think, according to the power that works within us, to Him be the glory in the church and in Christ Jesus to all generations forever and ever. Amen." (Ephesians 3:20–21)

Additional resources available from Call of Love Ministries include:

• *Dare to Connect* tool kit
• *The Simple Truth* book
• *Dare to Love* TV program
• *Dare to Ask* radio program
• Calloflove.org

Suggested Books to Read

Lesson 1

*Islam, Muhammad, & the Koran: A Documented Analysis, Labib Mikhail

Studies in the Sermon on the Mount , D. Martyn Lloyd-Jones

*Joshua: No Falling Words, Dale Ralph Davis

Lesson 2

*One God One Message, Paul D. Bramsen

The Case for Christ, Lee Strobel

The New Testament Documents: Are They Reliable?, F. F. Bruce

Lesson 3

*Being The Body, Charles Colson and Ellen S. Vaughn

*Unveiling Islam, Ergun M. Caner and Emir F. Caner

Lesson 4

Assured of Heaven, Robert S. Ricker

*Answering Islam: The Crescent in Light of the Cross, Norman L. Geisler
and Abdul Saleeb

Lesson 5

*The Grace Awakening, Charles R. Swindoll

*Islam: What Non Muslims Should Know, John Kaltner

Lesson 6

*The Prodigal God, Tim Keller

I Dared to Call Him Father. Richard H. Schneider

The Father Heart of God. Floyd McClung

Children of the Living God, Sinclair B. Ferguson

Lesson 7

Mere Christianity, by C.S. Lewis

Lesson 8

*The Truth About Islam & Women, by John Ankerberg and Emir Caner

Lesson 9

Out of the Saltshaker and Into the World, Rebecca Manley Pippert

*A Muslim's Heart, Edward J. Hoskins

Lesson 10

More Than a Carpenter, Josh McDowell

*Glad News! God Loves You My Muslim Friend, Samy Tanago

Lesson 11

Communion With the Triune God, John Owen

*One God One Message, Paul D. Bramsen

Lesson 12

The New Evidence that Demands a Verdict, Josh McDowell

*The Holiness of God, R.C. Sproul

*Answering Islam: The Crescent in Light of the Cross, Norman L. Geisler and Abdul Saleeb

Note: All books with asterisks (*) are available for you to order through www.calloflove.org. Look for the other books online, or in your local Christian bookstore.

Glossary

Allah The name of the god of Islam.

Awra The Encyclopedia of Islam defines awrah as pudendum, that is "the external genitals, especially of the female (Latin pudendum [literally] a thing to be ashamed of)." The World Book Dictionary 'Uloum ed-Din by Ghazali, Dar al-Kotob al-'Elmeyah, Beirut , Vol II, Kitab Adab al-Nikah, p. 65.

Carnelian A pale to deep red or reddish-brown variety of clear chalcedony (quartz), precious stones.

Ebonites Or *Ebionites*; Heretical sect that appeared in early Christianity and which some Muslims claimed to be true Christians. They did not believe that Jesus was the Son of God. They also held to the observance of the Jewish law with some variations.

Gnostic Applied to various early Christian sects that claimed direct personal knowledge beyond the Gospel or the church hierarchy. The adjective meaning "relating to knowledge" (lowercase "g") is from 1656.

Hadith A written report of a saying or deed. The Hadith collections are the most important models of Muhammad's words and deeds for Muslims to follow.

Huras Or *Huris*; The virgins in the Muslim Paradise who serve the faithful (men). Seventy-two Huris will be the portion for each Muslim man who dies as a martyr or while fighting for the cause of Allah. They are described as being extremely beautiful with black wide eyes. They are not human women, but creatures prepared specifically for paradise.

Imam Islamic leader; spiritual head of the Muslims; leader of prayer in the mosque. Also called Sheik.

Janna Or *Jannah*; the Muslim paradise as described in the Qur'an.

Jihad Striving, struggling, and endeavoring. Commonly translated as *Holy War*.

Jizya	Or *Jizyah*; The poll-tax or rather "protection money" that has to be paid by the Christians and Jews living under Islamic rule, who refuse to convert to Islam.
Ka'bah	Or *Kabah, Kaabah*; the cube-like building in the center of the mosque in Mecca. Muslims are to face it during ritual prayer (salat). It contains the black stone which is supposedly sent from heaven. The Kabah is said to be directly below the throne of God, therefore Mecca is considered the navel of the world. Muslims believe that the Kabah was first built by Adam but was destroyed in the flood. It is also supposed to have been built by Abraham and Ishmael (Sura 2:127). However, historical data contradicts this belief, as none of them ever went to Mecca (http://www.answering-islam.org/Index/index.html).
Khalif	Or *Caliph*; a leader of an Islamic group, regarded as a successor to Muhammad.
Mahr	Bridal money given by the husband to his wife at the time of marriage.
Manumitted	Released or set free from slavery.
Pantheon	The gods of a particular country or group of people.
Pillars of Islam	The five religious practices that Muslims observe to gain favor before Allah.
Qur'an	*Koran* or *Quran*; also called Al-furqan and al-Mushaf. The book that Muslims believe was given to Muhammad by Allah.
Quraysh	The tribe that Muhammad belonged to. The tribe that was the custodian of the Ka'aba before Islam.
Ramadan	The ninth and holiest month of Muslim calendar. It was in this month that the Qur'an was supposed to have been sent down.
Sadaqah	A commendable and voluntary giving.
Shari'a Law	Islamic law, considered the divine law.

Shia'	Or *Shiites*; meaning "followers," "members of the party." The second largest Muslim sect, they follow Ali, son-in-law of Muhammad.
Sufis	The mystical movement within Islam that began in the eighth or ninth century.
Sunnis	Or *Sunna*; the largest of the Muslim sects, rivals to the Shiites.
Sura	Or *Surah*; Arabic word meaning "copy"; a chapter of the Qur'an.
Syncretize	To combine differing elements or beliefs, especially with partial success or a heterogeneous result.
Umma	The nation or community of Islam worldwide.
Wa'ad	The pagan ritual of burying female infants alive, practiced in the Arabian Peninsula.
Wadud	Arabic adjective meaning amicable, friendly.
Wahhabi	A fundamentalist form of Islam, especially prevalent in Saudi Arabia.
Yahweh	Or *Yah-wah*; one of the names of God in the Bible, represented in Hebrew by the tetragrammaton ("four letters") יהוה (*Yod Heh Vav Heh*), transliterated into Roman script *Y H W H*. Because it was considered blasphemous to utter the name of God it was only written and never spoken. This resulted in the original pronunciation being lost. The name may have originally been derived from the old Semitic root הוה (*hawah*) meaning "to be" or "to become" (www.behindthename.com).
Zakat	Required, legal, and obligatory charity of a Muslim. One of the five pillars of Islam.
Zoroastrianism	A religion in Persia founded in 600 BC by Zoroaster, the principal beliefs of which are in the existence of a supreme deity, Ahura Mazda, and in a cosmic struggle between a spirit of good and a spirit of evil.

Leader's Guide

Thank you for choosing *Dare to Explore* for your group. Our prayer is that this study will be a blessing, and that it will strengthen the faith of every participant.

At the end of this journey together, you will:

- Know the truth about Islam.
- Be aware of the spread of Islam in America.
- Be able to make a comparison between Islamic beliefs and true Christian Faith.
- Be equipped with practical ways to reach Muslims in your community.
- Be capable of addressing some of the difficult questions that Muslims commonly ask Christians.
- Possess trusted resources for more in-depth studies to help you grow in your faith as well as learn more about Islam.
- Have a more explicable biblical foundation on the subjects discussed.
- Highlight specific Bible and Qur'an passages in your discussions with Muslims.

In order to make the most of this Bible study, please read the Introduction. The Introduction includes guidelines on where to find certain needed information. We encourage you to read it with your group in the first week of study.

Lesson Structure

The lessons in *Dare to Explore* are intended to be read and prepared individually by every participant during the week, then discussed together at a weekly group meeting. Below is a guide to the different parts of the lesson. You can share this information with your group so that they will know the structure of each lesson, its different sections, and the homework expected of them. This is a suggested guide, but feel free to tailor the study to the particular needs of your group.

1. **Islam:** This section includes academic information about Islam. Most lessons are separated into Part I and Part II to help the reader categorize the material and understand it better. The material presented in this section is taken from trusted resources mentioned at the end of each lesson.

2. **Answers from the Word of God:** This section takes us back to our own

Christian beliefs. What does the Word of God say about what was presented in the Islam section? Does our faith agree or disagree with Islam? This section is divided into several parts:

Side Trip: The Side Trip is designed to help the participant depend on the Word of God as the ultimate source to identify a principle, define a word or explain a certain belief. For clarity, and to aid in comparisons it is presented as a table. This focal point's subject is separate from the following sections. It is considered an additional Side Trip that will address something mentioned in the Islam section.

Main Trip: This is the heart of the biblical part of the lesson. One topic is chosen in each lesson to be thoroughly discussed, both on a general and personal level. The Bible passage that will be studied is included at the beginning of each Main Trip, except where the passage is a full chapter.

Probing Deeper. This is where the participant will answer some questions from both the section on Islam and the Main Trip. There are five questions: The first question is always an easy light one, with the last two questions becoming more personal.

Rest on the Road. This section encourages the participant to talk to God and express his or her concerns and worries, and to give thanks.

3. **Points of Interest:** This section offers additional resources for the moderator and the participants such as Bible passages to look up, books to read, and websites to search.

How to Lead or Moderate the Lessons

The following method of study has been tried with *Dare to Explore*, and the results have been highly positive. These forms helped participants enjoy studying the lessons on their own during the week, and equipped them to come to the group sessions ready to participate through comments, personal reflections, and questions.

We have created three forms (on pages 167-169) for you to use.

- **Form I: Setting Personal Goals** (page 167)
  This form will help the participants define the expectations and goals before beginning *Dare to Explore*. At the conclusion of the study, looking back over the responses listed will help the leader and the participant evaluate if the weeks spent in study met their goals and answered all of their questions.

  Give a copy of Form I to each participant at the first meeting to fill out and give back to you. Hold on to these copies, so you can discuss them

with the group after the twelve lessons are completed.

- **Form II: Weekly Summary Assignments** (page 168)
  Every week five different people will sign up on this sheet for the five different sections of each lesson. They will be responsible to summarize the section they signed up for. For example the person who takes the assignment of Islam part I will read that part at home and be ready to present to the group a summary of what the section says. The same applies to Islam Part II, Side Trip, and Main Trip. The leader keeps this form.

- **Form III: Sign-up Reminder** (page 169)
  Give these paper slips to the participants as a reminder of what they signed up for that week. Print this form on colored paper and encourage your group to use them as bookmarks during the study.

Assigning the four parts of each lesson to different people in the group will encourage them to prepare, participate, and reflect on the information before they come to class. This exercise will also help stimulate productive and thoughtful feedback from group members. Group members not assigned a section summary are encouraged to add their own comments or ask questions before the class moves from one part of the lesson to the next. The leader should be ready to fill in for anyone who signed up for a summary, but can't make it to the study, or didn't have time to prepare.

Reading the actual lesson word for word in class is discouraged because it will not give the opportunity for discussion and questions unless the group is willing to meet for two hours of reading together before discussing the lesson.

Ninety minutes is the ideal amount of time to spend on each lesson with a group that has prepared ahead of time.
- Opening prayer and welcome
- Islam Part I: Summarized by one participant followed by comments and questions
- Islam Part II: Summarized by one participant followed by comments and questions
  - If you are using the accompanying videos watch all the segments through the group question here.
- Side Trip: Bible verses read and summary of outcome shared and discussed
- Main Trip: Summary and leader's comments with any questions
- Probing Deeper: Give group members the opportunity to share their answers if they are comfortable. If you find that the questions have already been covered earlier in discussion feel free to skip any of them
  - If you are using the accompanying videos watch the second part of the lesson here.

- Prayer: Encourage participants to pray out loud, meditating on the Rest on the Road portion of the lesson
- Sign-ups for next week: Pass out the sign-up sheet (Form II) for next week's lesson and make sure that five people sign up for the five sections of the lesson. Encourage those who do not normally participate to sign up for a section they would be comfortable summarizing. The Side Trip sections may be the best portions of the study to start a less vocal group member on.

Make sure you have enough copies of each form. Additional copies to print are available online at www.calloflove.org or request them by e-mail at info@ calloflove.org

If you need help answering a question, please e-mail (info@calloflove.org) and one of the writers will send you the answer with helpful resources before your next lesson.

Please be sure to read the Introduction (page vii) with your group before you begin your study. Also please read the Leader's Guide provided at the end of the book so you will understand how each section of the lesson works (page 163).

Remember that you are the moderator of your group and you are helping each person learn how to study and process the information. Be alert for any non-biblical teachings or suggestions while participants are sharing, and always use passages from the Bible to correct, explain, or confirm a teaching.

Try to send a reminder e-mail (or call those without e-mail) at least two days before each meeting so people will have time to read, prepare, and pray. Encourage those who may not be able to attend to let you know ahead of time in case you need to find someone else to summarize a portion of the lesson.

Most importantly, pray for your group during the week; pray while you are preparing to teach, and pray during the lesson. May the Lord give you His wisdom as you lead.

Form I
Setting Personal Goals

Name _____

Email (optional) _____

Why did you choose to study *Dare to Explore*?

_____

_____

Please check the three most important for you:

☐ Know the truth about Islam.

☐ Be aware of the spread of Islam in America.

☐ Be able to make a comparison between Islamic beliefs and True Christian Faith.

☐ Be equipped with practical ways to reach Muslims in your community.

☐ Be capable of addressing some of the common difficult questions that Muslims ask.

☐ Possess trusted resources for more in-depth studies to grow in your faith and to learn more about Islam.

☐ Have a more explicable biblical foundation on the subjects discussed.

☐ Highlight specific Bible and Qur'an passages in your discussions with Muslims.

Form II
Weekly Summary Assignments Group Name: _____

	Islam Part I	Islam Part II	Side Trip	Main Trip
Lesson 1 Date:				
Lesson 2 Date:				
Lesson 3 Date:				
Lesson 4 Date:				
Lesson 5 Date:				
Lesson 6 Date:				
Lesson 7 Date:				
Lesson 8 Date:				
Lesson 9 Dagte:				
Lesson 10 Dat:				
Lesson 11 Date:				
Lesson 12 Date:				

Form III
Assignment Reminders

Dare to Explore Bible Study Assignment Reminder

Name: _____

My responsibility for group session date: ____ / ____ / ____   Lesson #_____

Summarize (*circle one*):   Islam Part I   Islam Part II   Side Trip   Main Trip

---

Dare to Explore Bible Study Assignment Reminder

Name: _____

My responsibility for group session date: ____ / ____ / ____   Lesson #_____

Summarize (*circle one*):   Islam Part I   Islam Part II   Side Trip   Main Trip

---

Dare to Explore Bible Study Assignment Reminder

Name: _____

My responsibility for group session date: ____ / ____ / ____   Lesson #_____

Summarize (*circle one*):   Islam Part I   Islam Part II   Side Trip   Main Trip

---

Dare to Explore Bible Study Assignment Reminder

Name: _____

My responsibility for group session date: ____ / ____ / ____   Lesson #_____

Summarize (*circle one*):   Islam Part I   Islam Part II   Side Trip   Main Trip

We would like to hear from you

We prepared *Dare to Explore* with the hope of introducing you to the journey of ministering to Muslims, while at the same time strengthening your own faith. We hope that while taking this Bible Study the Holy Spirit has started to work in your heart. We would appreciate knowing how this Bible Study helped you. Please check the box that applies to you:

❑ This is the first time I have been introduced to the concept of salvation and I have decided to accept Jesus Christ as Lord and Savior.

❑ I am still not sure if I am a child of God.

❑ I am a believer but am still unsure of my ability to share my faith with Muslims.

❑ As a true follower of Christ, my heart was filled with love towards Muslims and a yearning to reach them with the good news.

We encourage you to talk to your group leader about any doubts you may still have concerning your faith, or your ability to share that faith. Still looking for more answers? Contact us at the website listed below and tell us what's on your mind, or mail this form.

If you are interested in more information about Call of Love, or how you can reach Muslims, we would be glad to send you more information. If you are able to support Call of Love through prayers or donations, please check a box below. You may also contact us through our website: **www.calloflove.org**, or at **info@calloflove.org**.

❑ I need more information about how to reach Muslims for the Lord

❑ I will support Call of Love through prayer

❑ I have enclosed a donation to Call of Love

Your Name:_____

Address: _____

City: _____ State: _____ Zip Code _____

Tel: (_____) _____ Email: _____

Mail this form to: Call of Love Ministries, P.O. Box 498698, Cincinnati, OH 45249

Evaluation

Thank you for your willingness to share your comments with us. This will help us in our future Bible Study writings. Please fill the line in front of each question with a number corresponding to your experience using a scale of 1 to 10; 10 = Excellent and 1 = Very poor.

Islam Section

____ Was this section understandable?

____ Were all unfamiliar words defined?

____ Were there too many or too few details about the subject?

General comments for this section: _____

_____

_____

Side Trip Section

____ Did this section enrich the study?

____ Did the Bible passages used make sense to you?

General comments for this section: _____

_____

_____

Main Trip Section

____ Was the spiritual topic covered thoroughly?

____ Was the section organized and easy to understand?

____ Did this section provide too much or too little in explanation of the Biblical truth?

General comments for this section: _____

_____

_____

Probing Deeper Section

____ Were five questions a reasonable number?

____ Were the questions appropriate for the lesson?

____ Was the wording clear?

General comments for this section: _____

_____

_____

(continued on next page)

Rest on the Road

____ Did you think this is a good closing for each lesson?

____ Did you use this as part of the group sharing or only for personal study?

General comments for this section: _____

_____

_____

Points of Interest

____ Were the Bible passages, books, and websites suggested helpful?

Overall comments and notes:

Would you be comfortable in encouraging other groups or churches to study *Dare to Explore?* ____ Yes ____ No

Any other comments we need to know:_____

_____

_____

_____

_____

_____

Your Name (optional):_____

Address:_____

City: _____ State: _____ Zip Code _____

Tel: (_____) _____ Email: _____

Please mail your evaluation to:
Call of Love Ministries, P.O. Box 498698, Cincinnati, OH 45249

Or go online and fill in the same evaluation:
www.calloflove.org/dte/

CPSIA information can be obtained
at www.ICGtesting.com
Printed in the USA
FFOW02n1117020216

9 781613 797488